DEVELOPING FAITH

DEVELOPING FAITH

Lesson Plans for Senior High Religion Classes

Kieran Sawyer, S.S.N.D.

Ave Maria Press ~ Notre Dame, Indiana 46556

Nihil Obstat:

Rev. Richard Breitbach
Censor Librorum

Published with Ecclesiastical Permission.

© 1978 by Ave Maria Press, Notre Dame, Indiana, 46556

Library of Congress Catalog Card Number: 78-72942
International Standard Book Number: 0-87793-164-X

Printed and bound in the United States of America.

Table of Contents

Introduction

How to Use This Book

The lesson plans in this book have a wide variety of uses. Individual units, singly or in combination, can be used as the basis for an entire semester course with senior high students in a school or a parish religious education setting. The units or individual lessons might also be used to introduce or to supplement a course based on another text or program. Many of the activities in the lessons can be adapted for use in teen retreats, communal penance services, Christian living experiences, etc. A culling of the key lessons from each unit could provide the basis for an intensive confirmation preparation course. The material can also be adapted for lectures and workshops for adults.

The lessons were developed "on the job" over a period of several years, for day-to-day use in various kinds of situations. It is to be emphasized that the material as presented here was designed to be used with senior high students, especially sophomores, either in school or parish programs. Junior high teachers who wish to use the lessons should carefully select and adapt only what is suitable to the maturity level of the younger teen. It is better not to use this material in junior high if the students are likely to encounter it as part of a senior high program.

Method and Aim

The method employed in these lessons is geared to the level of religious and psychological growth of the average 15 to 18-year-old. It seems a necessary part of adolescent development that youngsters question and challenge the value systems they have been taught since infancy. This seemingly negative conduct is part of a total process of appropriation and interiorization in which young persons sift, weigh, and test the values of their society to determine which of these they will take with them into adulthood. The catechesis of adolescents is geared toward supporting the young person as he or she works through that difficult process. The goal of adolescent catechesis is that the young people will eventually appropriate and make a commitment to the total faith system known as Catholic Christianity.

The overall aims of this program, therefore, are to help adolescents:

—to deepen their personal response to God; to grow in an awareness of themselves as individuals who are loved by God and who are called to respond to his love.

—to clarify their own religious and moral values; to understand their personal beliefs and convictions and to work through their doubts and confusions.

—to appropriate Catholic Christianity—to make a personal decision to accept the faith they have inherited from their parents and to live according to its challenges.

The method used to accomplish these aims is a combination of dialogue, input, and actual experience.

Dialogue

Dialogue (or discussion) is the first essential element of the method. Adolescents often do not know what they really think or what they believe about matters of faith. One way they can discover their own ideas is by expressing them. Therefore they must be given a chance to articulate their doubts as well as their beliefs, their questions as well as their developing answers. Such articulation helps the young persons to clarify things in their own minds. It also gives the catechist invaluable insights into the faith growth that has already taken place in the life of the individual student and the group, and it points out areas that need clarification or strengthening.

As catechists of adolescents it is one of our most important tasks to establish an atmosphere in which this kind of honest dialogue is possible. The basic ingredient of such an atmosphere is trust—a mutual attitude of respect that characterizes all of the relationships that make up the teaching-learning situation. As catechists this means, first of all, we must trust the *young people* we are working with; we must really believe in their honesty and basic goodness as human beings. We must be ready to really listen to their opinions and questions and convey by the manner in which we do so, a sense of acceptance and respect.

As catechists we must also believe in *ourselves* as mature human beings. We must not allow ourselves to be personally threatened by the doubts and problems of the teens, and must be willing to be truthful and open with them about our own convictions and questions. Finally, and most importantly, we must have a firm trust in *God* himself who is always present in the catechetical situation. Ultimately he will touch the hearts of these young people and draw them to himself.

In an atmosphere of mutual trust the catechist is able to encourage the faith growth of the adolescents, and also to challenge them to think more deeply, to discover the inconsistencies in their own value systems, and to be alert for any discrepancy in their lives between what they say they believe and what they actually do.

A dialogue session of this kind requires—as does every lesson—preparation. The values clarification techniques developed by Sid Simon and his associates are valuable aids in helping young people to think critically about themselves and their own values, and to share their ideas in a group. Anyone using these lesson plans should be familiar with Simon's book, *Values Clarification: A Handbook of Practical Strategies for Teachers and Students* (New York: Hart Publishing Co., 1972). References to *Values Clarification* will be made throughout the text. Also recommended is *Values and Teaching* by Louis Raths, Merrill Harmin, and Sid Simon (Columbus, Ohio: Charles Merrill, 1966). References to this book will also be given in the lessons.

One of the most valuable strategies presented in these books is the "open question" technique with its corresponding "pass privilege." The open question concept states that the teacher is free to ask a student any question about any aspect of the student's life or values—nothing is too personal or too private, too trivial or too important to be asked. The pass privilege concerns answering such questions. The person of whom a question is asked always has two options: to answer the question honestly and openly, or to pass. It is not desirable for the student to give the answer the teacher wants to hear. A "pass" answer is a non-answer. It means whatever the passer wants it to mean: Go away, I'm tired; I don't know; Let me think about it; That's not something I feel I can share; What a stupid question, etc. The student is also free to turn the question back to the teacher, or to refer it to another student. The pass privilege would, of course, also apply to the new people being questioned.

This is a delicate and powerful technique. It will work only if the teacher deeply respects the young people he or she is questioning. Once the teens realize that their ideas and opinions will be listened to and valued, they will be very open in answering the questions posed. The teacher should remind them often of their right to pass, and should accept a pass answer just as he or she would accept any other response—with respect.

One of the more dramatic uses of the open question technique is the "public interview."[1] A volunteer is interviewed by the teacher on some important area of life that is interesting to the class. For instance students being interviewed can be asked for their beliefs about teenage alcoholism, attendance at Sunday Mass, when and how they pray. The public interview helps students to understand one another and to see the beauty and complexity in the lives of their companions. It demonstrates that students can talk honestly about their thoughts and experiences, even deeply personal ones, with a group that is supportive and non-judgmental. Moreover, the listeners often discover that sharing in another's ideas and values opens up alternatives that are worth considering for their own lives.

The authors of *Values and Teaching* point out emphatically the kind of atmosphere needed for such value sharing techniques to be effective:

> Needless to say, a public interview must be carried out in a classroom in which there is acceptance, security, and warmth. There can be no judging, certainly no ridicule. What we get is a glimpse of a real life, a life that must be respected. All our lives have both beauty and blemishes, and we use the public interview to raise some of this to the surface, to look at it, and to learn from it. The public interview is an effective technique for bringing more humanness into the classroom.[2]

Input

The second key element in the method used in these lessons is *input*. The adolescent needs a clear, concise presentation of the cognitive truths of the faith. This is especially true for today's teens whose formal religious training has been profoundly affected by the catechetical transition of the past 10 years. For many, their catechesis has been sporadic and uneven; often the pastors, teachers, and parents responsible for their early religious formation were attempting to use materials and methods the rationale and spirit of which they did not fully understand or agree with.

The preliminary discussion opening each unit helps the teacher discover just what the students know, what ideas they are confused about, what areas of knowledge seem to be

[1]See *Values Clarification*, p. 139. *Values and Teaching*, pp. 142–149.
[2]*Values and Teaching*, p. 145.

entirely lacking, and what negative attitudes need to be overcome. Input lessons should be carefully prepared to accord with this analysis of the particular group's strengths and weaknesses. The material in the input sessions should be treated academically, with the students expected to keep accurate notes, to do supplementary readings and written reports, and to master the cognitive content for future testing and grading. It should, at the same time, be treated personally. The input material should thus become the basis for in-depth class discussions in which the students are encouraged to respond to the concepts in the lessons by applying them to their own life situations, by affirming their belief in them, and by raising further questions.

Experience

The third key element in the method is *experience*. Teens have to *do* their religion as well as study and discuss it. The total religion program must include built-in opportunities for private and group prayer, for meaningful celebrations of eucharist, penance, baptismal renewal and/or confirmation, for overnight or weekend retreats, and for community service and social action. The teens themselves should always help to plan these activities, and should discuss and evaluate them after taking part in them.

Additional Pointers

The lesson plans in this book are intended to be used creatively, not followed slavishly. Teachers are encouraged to adapt the materials to their own catechetical situation, to add to them, to select from them, to use them as springboards for new ideas. Remember that each group of adolescents will have different needs and questions.

The teacher should read through the entire set of lessons before he or she attempts to use any of them. Techniques presented in the earlier lessons are not explained again, and concepts taught in one lesson are often based on those developed in another.

The teacher should be completely comfortable with the material and techniques of a particular lesson before trying it with the students. The success of the lessons will depend largely on how well the teacher has assimilated the ideas and problems it contains. The teens must feel as though the questions and presentation are coming from the teacher, not from the lesson plan book.

Each unit has been divided into several sessions, but the division is somewhat arbitrary. The material in one lesson may keep a class involved for several hours, or it may take less than one hour. There is also some overlapping from lesson to lesson: sometimes the same material is taught in two completely different ways. Both lessons may be used, if it is felt that the students need the repetition, or the lesson best suited to the particular class can be chosen.

Several sample handout sheets are included in the text. Permission is granted to duplicate these—for classroom use only. Copies of the lessons themselves, however, should **not** be given to the students, nor should the discussion questions. Rather the teacher should present the material, idea by idea, allowing for flexibility in the natural flow of conversation and questioning.

It is strongly recommended that the students keep notebooks in which they record the key ideas of discussion sessions and the material presented in the input sessions. The notebook helps the students to see the continuity of a unit; moreover, the material from a previous lesson is at hand if the teacher wants to refer to it again. The teacher may also want the students to write in their notebooks a summary of and response to each session. These reaction statements serve as an important source of feedback for both teacher and student.

Above all it is to be remembered that the ideas and questions of the students are an essential ingredient for every session. Feedback techniques (based on values clarification strategies[3]) are included in most of the lessons.[4] Even when they are not included, the teacher should take time often to find out where the students stand on the topic being discussed, what questions they have, what they find disturbing, and what impression the lesson is making. The success of these lessons will depend largely on the ability of the catechist to get the students to communicate honestly—with the teacher, with one another, and ultimately with God.

[3]*Values Clarification*, pp. 163, 166, 241, 252, 385.
[4]A list of sample sentence starters for introductory or feedback sessions is found on page 103.

Unit One
Introductory Sessions

Faith and Prayer

The sessions in this unit are meant to help teens assess the growth of their faith and to come to a deeper understanding of God's presence in their lives. The sessions should also prove helpful in establishing the atmosphere of mutual respect and sharing which will be needed to implement the method in this book.[1] The sessions introduce both the teacher and the students to some of the main strategies and techniques that will be used throughout the lessons.[2]

The unit could be used in its entirety as a short course on prayer, faith, and the experience of God. Or the individual sessions (especially sessions 1, 2, 3, and 10) could be used separately as openers for any course or teen event in which the teacher wants to help the students to get in touch with their own life in relationship to God.

Session 1

A. Tell the class you are going to introduce them to four sophomores (or juniors or seniors). Place on a continuum[3] on the board the names:

    Casper—Hilary—Zady—Brutus

Describe each character in terms of his or her attitude toward religion.

    Caspar - Totally negative attitude toward religious things.
               Hates religion classes.
               Never goes to church if he can help it.
               Fights with his parents about religion.

[1]See introduction, pp. 2 and 3; and *Values and Teaching*, pp. 168ff.
[2]See *Values Clarification*, pp. 13–27.
[3]*Values Clarification*, p. 116. *Values and Teaching*, p. 129. A continuum is a method of looking at the full range of alternatives on a given question. Most issues are not a simple matter of black and white, but offer a spectrum of positions ranging from black to white. A continuum helps overcome and/or encourages the individual to see that his or her way of looking at an issue is only one among many possible options. The continuums given on pages 116–126 of *Values Clarification*, can be used very profitably to brighten up a dull Monday or to fill in 10 minutes of leftover class time.)

Hilary - Sees religion as unimportant, a bore.

So-what attitude toward religion classes.

Misses Mass if he can get away with it without a family squabble.

Seldom prays except when in trouble.

Zady - Does what is expected of him religiously.

Attends Mass regularly because his parents do.

Wants to get good grades in theology so studies hard.

Believes what he has been taught about religion and morality.

Brutus - Has made his own decision to be a Catholic Christian.

Attends Mass regularly because he wants to do that for God.

Prays often, in his own way, in his own words.

Wants to be a better Christian than he is, wants to learn more about God and his religion.

(Be sure to emphasize that Brutus is not a saint, a goody-two-shoes, or a Jesus freak. He is a normal teenager who has made his own commitment to Christianity. Zady, on the other hand, is still operating on his parents' values.[4])

B. Discuss:

* How do you explain why each of the four persons is where he is on the line?
* What were some of the influences in their lives that have led to these positions? (List these on the board. They would include family, friends, school, former religion classes, parish, pastors, etc.)
* Would kids in a Catholic high school rate higher or lower on the line than kids in a public high school?
* How should the religion teacher approach each of these people?
* I know families that have all four kinds of persons within one family. How would you explain that?
* What would an adult Caspar be like? Hilary? Zady? Brutus?
* What would it be like to have parents who were Caspars?, or parents like one of the others?

C. Pass out small slips of paper. Ask each student to write on the paper the name of the person on the continuum who most closely represents his own position.

Collect slips. Before tallying, have students guess where they think the majority of the class will be.

Tally slips and discuss results. (Some of the questions listed under B above may be kept to discuss at this time, after the tallying.)

D. Open questions or public interviews.[5]

In this technique the teacher may ask the student any question about any aspect of his life or values. If the student answers the question, he must answer honestly. However, if he does not want to answer any of the questions the teacher poses, he simply says "I pass." The option to pass must be respected by the teacher, who may then either ask another question or move to another student.

[4]See Unit 2.
[5]Values Clarification, p. 139 and 158.

Review the open question rules. Then ask each student in turn to explain what position he is on the Caspar-Brutus continuum and why.

Other questions that can be posed to the student on the floor include:

- How does your position now compare to your position last year? Two years ago?
- Would you say you are moving up or down the scale? Why?
- What was the greatest influence on your present position?
- Where do you think you'll be 10 years from now?
- Are you satisfied with your present position?
- Would you date a Caspar? Marry one?
- Which would you prefer to marry, a Catholic Hilary or a Lutheran Brutus?
- Would you be comfortable in a group of Caspars? Brutuses?
- Do you think you would be someplace else on the scale if you were going to a public (Catholic) school?

E. Written assignment:

Write a brief essay explaining how each of these things have affected your position on the *continuum*: family, friends, parish, grade school, religious training, etc.

Note: If D above is kept for a second session, this assignment could be given after C.

Alternate Session 1

A. Ask each student to complete the statement (in writing):

A religious person is one who . . .

Share answers and compile one definition of a religious person. Write this on the board.

B. Ask the students to rate themselves as a religious person, using their own definition as a standard, by placing themselves on a scale from one to four.

C. Share answers using the open question technique and questions like those listed above.

Session 2 — Who is your God?

A. Put one student's name on the board, e.g. Jim.

Discuss the difference between Dad's Jim, Mom's Jim, the teacher's Jim, his best friend's Jim, his girl friend's Jim.

Point out that Jim is one person, but each person who knows him has a little different experience of him.

B. Compare this to the experience of God. There is one God, but each of us has a different experience of him, so that Jim's God is not exactly the same as Mary's God, or my God.

C. Write an essay entitled "Who Is My God?"
The essay should describe your God, tell how you got to know him, what he is like, what he thinks of you, how often you think about him, how much time you spend with him, etc.

Session 3 — Spending time with God

A. Look around the room and find two students who are sitting quite near one another but are obviously not sitting together. Say "Jim, have you spent any time with Lori since you came into this room? You mean you could be sitting two feet away from her and not spend any time with her? Could you spend time with someone sitting on the other side of the room? in another room? What does it mean to spend time with someone?"

B. Ask class: Did you spend any time with God this week? Could you go to Mass and not spend time with God? Write on board: Prayer is spending time with God. Discuss the meaning of this definition.

C. Pair up with a friend you can talk to. Read assignments from Session 2 to each other. Ask your partner at least two questions about what he or she has written.

D. Public interviews[6]

Ask for a volunteer who will sit at the teacher's desk or lectern. Interview him using the questions listed below. Be sure to remind him of the "pass" privilege. When the interview is over, he may select the next person to be interviewed, or he may become the interviewer if he wishes. (If it is early in the year, and the students do not know each other or the teacher well, it would probably be better for the teacher to do all of the interviews to maintain the proper attitude of respect and openness.) Take plenty of time with this exercise. It is an excellent way to get to know the students and to show them that you mean to be nonjudgmental in your approach to their ideas.

How did you picture God when you were little? Now?

What do you think heaven will be like? Hell?

What do you remember from religion classes in grade school?

Are you happy about the religious training you received from your parents? Will you give your children the same kind of training?

How much time do you spend with God? Do you pray in your own words or use church prayers?

How well do you know God as a person?

If you could talk to God right now, what would you say to him?

Session 4 — Ways of experiencing God

A. It will help us to understand our experience of God if we have a better understanding of the way we experience our own parents.

We experience our parents in various ways:

1 - The Providers—This is the dominant experience of parents for most children. Have the students list some of the things their parents provide. Be sure to include non-material things.

2 - The Wonder-Workers—Think back to when you were four or five years old. Parents were all-powerful, all-knowing beings. List some of the "wonderful" things they knew, they could do. (Tie shoes, heal owies, read the paper.)

[6]*Values Clarification*, p. 139; *Values and Teaching* p. 142.

3 - The Bosses or Moral Guides—Parents tell us what to do, how to live, what is right and what is wrong. They are the guides, the lawgivers, the disciplinarians, and the punishers. Discuss whether this is a positive or negative experience of parents.

4 - The Nobodies or Enemies—Every young person eventually has to separate himself from his parents if he is to become a unique, free individual. Sometimes parents seem to get in the way of this, seem to tie the child down, restrict his freedom. This is the experience of many teenagers. They react by negating the parents. Parents no longer count; their opinions, their presence, their help are not wanted or appreciated.

5 - The Friends—The experience of friendship develops only after many years. Friendship is a relationship between equals, each needs the other, each can trust the other, each has something to give and something to gain. Discuss: When did you first start thinking of your mom or dad as a person other than as a parent; as someone with feelings and needs and fears, as someone who needed you as well as you needed her or him?

B. Though a child might experience its parents in any of the above ways at various times in its life, some of the experiences are associated with certain stages of psychological growth. Diagram at the board the relationship of child to parent. The outside circle represents the parental circle, the inside circle represents the child.

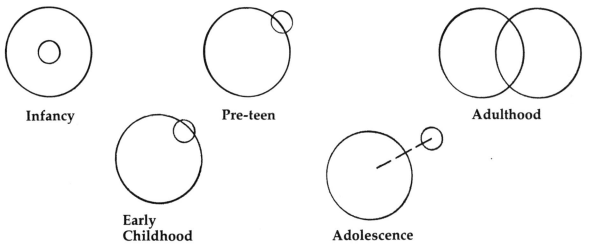

| Infancy | Pre-teen | Adulthood |
| Early Childhood | Adolescence | |

Infancy	Child is in the center of a protective, providing circle.
Childhood	Child is beginning to move out of circle. Parents are all-knowing, all-powerful beings who reward when good, punish when naughty.
Pre-teen	Child likes to spend time outside the family circle. Parents are law-givers and, of necessity, punishers.
Teen	Child gets as far from family circle as possible without breaking supply lines. Parents seem to get in the way. Teens know more than they do, want to do their own thing, be their own persons. Other relationships are more important than family.
Adult	The child, now an adult, sees parents as equals. Real friendship is now possible.

C. Look at the developing relationship from the parents' point of view. What would you do at each stage to show your children that you really love them and want to develop a friendship relationship with them?

D. Written assignment
Which of the five experiences above best characterizes your relationship with your parents right now? Explain.

Session 5 — The Experience of God (continued)

A. Ask the students to relate the various ways they experience their parents to the various ways people experience God. Help them to see that they have probably experienced God in most of these ways.

1 - God the Provider. We experience God as provider all the time, in rain, sunshine, good food, perfect days, friends, in whatever in life is for us. It is not necessary to be aware of the giver in order to experience the gift.

2 - God the Wonder-Worker, the Planner, the Power-in-Charge. When we study the intricacies of nature, of atoms, cells, galaxies, birth, the human body, we say "somebody had to plan that. It didn't just happen." If no one told us there is a creator greater than we, we would know it from the experience of the wonders of creation.

3 - God the Moral Guide, the Lawgiver, the Boss. Rightness and wrongness are bigger than any person, than all persons. If no one told you it is wrong to steal, how would you know it is wrong? (As soon as someone stole something from you.)

4 - God the Enemy, the Nobody. Sometimes the things God asks of us seem to be too much to take. It seems like God wants to destroy us or our freedom. We know God isn't a nobody but we wish he were. We wish he'd leave us alone; he demands too much. He seems unnecessary or contradictory. (Even Jesus experienced God in this way. When?)

5 - God the Father-Friend. Most teens have probably not experienced God as Friend, at least not to a high degree. To experience God as friend is to know with my whole being that he loves me, that he believes in me, that he expects me to be free, unique. God the friend can depend on me. He can give me responsibility, entrust others to my care.

B. Write and/or discuss:

Which of the five above best expresses your experience of God?

C. Ask: Is it possible that anyone might not have experienced God at all? (Probably not, but a person might not be aware that what he was experiencing was God.)

To explain the difference between experiencing and being aware of the person behind the experience use this example: You come home from school to find that your mom has just baked a batch of chocolate chip cookies for the family. You can either stuff your pockets and your mouth and whistle out of the kitchen, or stuff your pockets and your mouth and be aware of your mom who went through a lot of time and trouble to give you this small gift. Only if you are aware will you respond to the gift with gratitude.

Discuss: How can we become more aware of God in each of the above experiences? (Taking time to be aware is what prayer is all about.) What kind of response would each experience call forth?

    Provider—gratitude and petition
    Wonder-Worker—praise and awe
    Guide—prayer for direction, sorrow
    Enemy—something like Christ's prayer in the garden
    Friend—a desire to spend time with God, to do things for him

D. Spend some time tonight being aware of God and responding to him in some way. (Give students a chance to talk about this next class.)

Session 6 — The Experience of God—Prayer Experience

A. Have the class meet in a chapel or church, or arrange the classroom so that it provides an atmosphere of prayer. (If the church is used, gather in a cozy corner so the students can sit around on the floor or on mats, not in pews.)

B. Prepare a slide show to fit the song "Wonderful World."[7] Flash the slides slowly, asking the students to be aware of God whose work is evident in each picture. As each slide is flashed, one student is called on to explain how the picture tells about God and/or to say a little prayer suggested by the slide. (This can be done by taking turns in the circle, or by just allowing spontaneous responses. If you choose the circle—which is easier on the students—be sure to allow them freedom to pass.)

When you have been through the slides in this manner, show them again, this time singing the song with them. (The class will be surprised to see how perfectly the pictures fit the song!)

C. When the prayer time is over, give the students a chance to respond to the experience. Did they find that it really helped them to pray? Would they like to do this kind of thing more often? Be sure to accept and respect any negative responses you receive.

Alternate Session 6 — Joe Wise Creed

A. Play for the students the Creed from the Joe Wise record *A New Day*.[8] It is a good idea to have the words on an overhead transparency or to give copies to the class.

B. Discuss the Creed. Why does Joe Wise express his belief in God using those kinds of things? What kind of experience of God does he seem to have had? What do the various phrases mean? How is this prayer like or unlike a traditional creed?

C. Have the class write down 10 things that they really believe in. Share lists.

D. Using their lists, and whatever writing or artistic talents they have, each student should prepare a creed. He or she may want to make it into a poster or banner, or put it on tape with a musical background as Wise did.

E. Prepare a prayer experience at which these creeds are shared. Keep them to use for the creed in future school or parish Masses.

---

[7]"Wonderful World," *People's Hymnal Vol. 1.* F.E.L., 1925 Pontius Avenue, Los Angeles, CA. 90025. If you don't have some slides of creation/nature/people of your own, you might write ROA Films, 1696 North Astor St., Milwaukee, Wis. 53202.
[8]NALR, 5119 North 19th Ave. Phoenix, Arizona 85015.

Session 7 — For a particularly negative or mixed-up group

A. Have students complete in writing the statement: My biggest problem about God is . . .

   As students share responses, jot down what each says in essence. This will be a good guide for you in preparing future classes.

B. List the statements below on the board. Have students indicate their degree of belief in each statement by giving a number on a scale:

   1 (weak belief) - 2 - 3 - 4 (strong belief)

   1. There is some kind of God.
   2. God really cares about me.
   3. God will get me in the end if I don't watch out.
   4. I really wish I had more faith in God.
   5. If I listened to God it would spoil all my fun.
   6. If I listened to God—knew he cared about me—my life would be happier.

C. Write an essay, "Me and My God", responding to these statements.

D. Discuss the tallying of the responses above and the essays.

Session 8 — Faith problems

A. Explain: You are a part of a great and beautiful plan, a plan including all people and the whole world. You are able to know truth, to sort out the rightness and wrongness of things. You can see that truth and goodness are greater than you are. You are able to love, you are meant for love. You see love as the deepest reality, as the solution of all problems.

   This mysterious reality within you—this plan, this truth, this love—is God. God himself is within you. Whenever you understand better what makes you you, you know God better. When you see the plan and beauty of your life and of creation, you are seeing God. When you say, "It is wrong to hurt another person. It is right to be free," you are expressing the truth of God that lives in you. When you really love, you will know that love is greater than anything a mere human being can experience. A real love experience is always an experience of God.

B. If all this is true, why don't you know it? If God is within you, speaking to you, why don't you hear him? Why is it so hard to believe? What are the obstacles to faith? Give the students a copy of the statements listed below. Have them write a short paragraph finishing the sentence starter: I am not as close to God as I should be because. . . They should complete the answer in their own words, or they may wish to use the words and phrases from the sample statements that seem to apply to themselves.

I am not as close to God as I should be because:

1) I don't take time to think about the deeper realities of life: who I am, where I fit in the world, what happens after death, what is really right and wrong.

2) I think about these things, but I don't relate the answers to God.

3) I want to be my own God. I don't want to have to be responsible to anyone but myself for what I do with my life.

4) I am afraid of facing God. He might not like me, or he might find fault with the way I am living my life. He might ask me to change something I don't want to change.

5) I have too many mixed up ideas about God. The God I experience doesn't fit in with God as I learn about him.

6) I don't need God. I can take care of myself.

Ask the class to share their answers. If this seems too threatening, collect them and read them aloud without identifying the authors.

(To make copies of this page, use duplicate in tear-out section at back of book.)

C. My role as teacher, your role as student, God's role in your faith life.

The teacher's role is to:

> Correct your mistaken ideas about God.
> Answer your questions if possible.
> Encourage you to let God speak within you.
> Provide a setting where you can share your understanding of God and your questions with each other.
> Try not to be another obstacle.

The student's role is to:

> Try to find your own place in this world.
> Take God and yourself seriously.
> Discover your own beliefs, your own set of values.

God's role is: God is a mysterious power within you who loves you and calls you to freedom. If you let him, God will tell you who he is.

D. Write an essay explaining: What seem to be the obstacles that keep you from believing in God? How serious are you about working these through? How do you see the roles explained above?

Session 9 — The Parable of the Three Art Teachers[9]

A. Tell the class the parable: Once upon a time there were three art teachers . . .

Teacher One—Letter-Perfect Lester: His art room was in perfect order. Had a place for everything and everything in its place. Showed you a sample painting and gave you a set of directions that showed you exactly how to make a painting like that. Walked around the room, watching how you were doing at following the directions. If you made a mistake, (for instance used red instead of green,) he put a big black X on your painting. You had to go to the shelf where the eradicator was kept and erase the X, then start over. Your grade depended on how well you followed directions. Too many X's and you flunked.

Teacher Two—Do-Your-Thing Delbert: Lester got sick at the quarter and the school hired Delbert. Room was a mess. Told you you could do whatever you wanted in his room, just so you didn't bother him. If you asked him for help in painting a tree, he'd say, "Just do your thing. You can paint that tree however you want to." Some worked hard and turned out beautiful paintings. Some tried hard, but couldn't produce much. One student sat in the corner all quarter and slept. Another decided his thing was messing up other people's things—he went around with a black marker and smeared up everyone else's work. The end of the quarter came and everybody in the whole class got an A in art, even the one who slept in every class and the one who messed up everyone's work.

Teacher Three—Free-Choice Fred: Delbert was fired. The new teacher's name was Fred. You walked in the first day to find that everyone had some kind of art materials on his or her desk: one had red paint, one had green, one had all the

9This makes excellent material for a session that includes the teens and their parents.

brushes, one had all the rags. Fred explained that each person was responsible for the material assigned and had to see to it that whoever needed that particular material got it. Fred had just two rules: you could paint whatever you wanted, but it had to be unique, it couldn't be like anyone else's; and all the paintings when they were finished were to be hung on the back wall to form a giant mural. Yours had to blend in with everyone else's. So you had to keep your eye on what the others were doing, but you had to be careful not to copy. Fred would walk around the room encouraging everyone, but he never offered help unless you wanted it. If you made a mistake, he would show you how to blend the mistake right into the painting so that the mistake itself added to the beauty of the whole. You were graded in the end on how well you kept the two rules. The only ones who flunked were those who quit and those who never asked for help.

B. Students should write which art teacher they would prefer, and why. Discuss these answers.

C. Explain that the art teachers were made up to represent the idea of God as he is seen by different people. Each detail in the parable was put in to stand for something about the idea of God. With that in mind, ask the students to decipher the parable: what is God like to those who see him as a Lester, a Delbert, a Fred?

D. When you are sure students understand the parable, have them get into small groups to work out the answers to the following questions:

    1. If God were like Lester (Delbert, Fred) how would he act toward you?

    2. How would you act toward him?

    3. What would he consider sinful?

    4. How would he act when you sinned?

    5. What would be the advantages of having a God like Lester? like Delbert? like Fred?

    6. What would be the disadvantages for each?

    7. Which would you prefer God to be?

    8. Which do you think he is?

    9. If you were God, and had the whole world to keep in order, which would you be? When you are in a position of responsibility over people younger than yourself, which are you?

    10. Which of the three best represents the way your parents deal with you? Which do you think represents best your parents' idea of God?

    11. Where do the 10 Commandments fit into each scheme? (They are obvious in Lester, absent in Delbert. In Fred they are implicit in his rule to make your painting blend in with everyone else's.)

    12. What do you think of Fred's idea to give everyone only one of the needed supplies and make that person responsible for distributing it? Wouldn't it be better just to give everyone what he needs himself?

E. Ask for volunteers to impersonate the three versions of God. Have them debate the best way to run the world. The teacher should moderate the debate throwing in questions like those above.

F. Have students write a description of the art teacher who would be a symbol of God as they see him. Include in the description how he gives orders, corrects errors, distributes materials, keeps order, rewards and punishes, and shows his love and concern.

Session 10 — Parable of the Unknown God

A. Distribute to the class copies of the poem on page 25. Read the poem to the students and ask for their reactions to it.

B. In discussing the poem ask questions like the following:

- Who are the Shula Hians? (The name is meant to be a take-off of High School, but it isn't necessary to the poem to know this.)
- How is the god in the poem like our God?
- How would you react if you were the god in the poem?
- What would you advise him to try next?
- Suppose there were a God trying to win your friendship, how would he have to go about it? What would he have to do to get through to you?

C. Someone is bound to suggest that the solution would be for the god to come to earth himself. Then ask:

- Should he take on a human form? Should he be rich or poor?
- Would the people believe him when he claimed to be a god?
- How would he get his desire for friendship across to them?
- Our God tried that, didn't he? What happened to him?
- What would happen if he tried it again?

Parable of the Unknown God

Once upon a mountaintop there lived
a kind and gentle god. In Shula Hi,
a village far below, his people lived.
They were a very busy people: many
books to read and many games to play,
and very many meetings to attend.

The Shula Hians seldom thought about
the kind and gentle god. So far away
he seemed. No one had ever seen his face.
Some doubted he was even there at all.

Yet, day by day the gentle god looked down
upon his own, and wanted very much
that they should be his friends. I must, he thought,
do some small thing to show them that I care.
And so each day he sent a messenger
to Shula Hi, a pack upon his back,
and in the pack he bore a special gift,
a gift for every person in the land.

Each day the gifts would come. Each day the people
ran with open arms to gather them.
But soon they grew quite used to being gifted.
Some began to grab gifts from the pack,
And some took more than they were meant to have,
and some complained of gifts that were too small.
At last no one remembered who the gifts
were from. And no one even thought to ask.

And far up on his mountaintop sat god.
Day after lonely day he waited
for a friendly word, a word of thanks, or just
a word that said, "Hi, god, I know you're there."

But no word came. The Shula Hians took
the gifts as if they had a right to them
and more. But god? Well, he was far away.
And some said, "What's he ever done for me?"
And some, "I don't believe he even is."

If I can't tell them that I am, god thought,
how can I tell that I am a friend
and want to give them friendship most of all?

And then his eyes lit up, "I know," he said,
"I'll give a party for my friends below.
I'll give a party and invite them all.
And surely if they spend some time with me,
and learn to know how much I really care,
oh, surely then they'll know I am their friend."

And so the invitations were sent out.
A list was posted on the town house wall
for all who wished to come to sign their names.

The Shula Hians saw the invitation.
Some just laughed and said, "That's not for me!"
And some said, "Spend a day with god? No way!"
And some were very busy with their chores
and said, "Some other time but not today."
And some were tempted: "Maybe it's for real,
and maybe god does want to be my friend."
And timidly they signed up for the day.
But when the others laughed they were ashamed
and found excuses why they couldn't go.

The party day arrived, but no one went.

And in his mountain home the kind god sat.
"I only want to give them love," he said.
"How can I tell them? Make them understand?
Is there not one who wants me for a friend?"

And in the village far below, the Shula Hians
laughed and cried and worked and played and died.
And seldom thought about the gentle god,
and did not know he loved them very much,
and did not know he loved . . . .
and did not know.

Sister Kieran Sawyer

(To make copies of this page, use duplicate in tear-out section at back of book.)

Unit 2

Values/Why We Do What We Do

This unit is designed to help adolescents understand their own psychological development, levels of motivation, and value systems. Many of the teen's "faith problems" are really growth problems—part of the normal process of moving from childhood into adulthood.

The concepts of Transactional Analysis (TA) are simple enough to be understood by teens and very helpful in supplying terminology and categories with which they can discuss their coming-to-maturity problems and successes. Only two sessions on TA are given here, but these could easily be expanded into a short unit. Texts and workbooks which expand on the use of TA with teens are available from other sources.

The sessions on moral development are a simplification of the moral stages of Lawrence Kohlberg. The three sessions given here could also be expanded in many ways.

Many of the lessons which come later in this book will be based on an understanding of the concepts developed in this short unit.

Session 1 — Parent, Child, Adult[1]

A. Show the book *I'm OK, You're OK* to the class and tell them that you are going to be presenting some of the ideas in Dr. Harris's book. Explain that in each of us there are three psychological persons, the parent, the child, and the adult. They are all present all the time, but they take turns running the show. In some of us one dominates most of the time, in others, another dominates.

> Child: In the child we find our *felt* reactions to life. The child is spontaneous, playful, creative. The child is also stubborn, demanding, and jealous. The child is best seen in a youngster under three years old, but is still very much alive at 13 and at 30.

[1]Sessions one and two are a much simplified presentation of the principles and terminology of Transactional Analysis. Some familiarity with this method of psychology is recommended before attempting to use the lessons. Recommended reading: Eric Berne, *Games People Play* (New York: Grove Press, 1964); Thomas Harris, *I'm OK, You're OK* (New York: Harper and Row, 1967.)

Parent: The psychological parent is the source of our *taught* concepts. Be careful in discussing this person not to confuse him with parents. The parent is part of you. All the rules and regulations about how to live are part of the parent. Most of these came from our parents, but we also absorbed many of them from other adults, from TV, and other sources. Parent formulas are: Shame on you, Never do that, Don't forget that, Watch out for.

Adult: The adult is the source of our *thought* concepts. In the adult we find reasoning, understanding, values, and ideals. The adult figures things out for himself. Dr. Harris says that the adult begins to develop in us already at age nine months. As soon as we see the reasons for things, they become part of the adult.

B. As an example use the case of a little child and something hot. Very early the rule is pounded into his little parent: Don't touch that. How does the child respond to such a rule? Right, he touches it at his first chance. But when he does touch it and gets hurt, he sees why he shouldn't touch the hot toaster. The rule "Don't touch the toaster" has now become part of his adult.

C. Present the material shown on the chart on p. 34. You may wish to teach the chart briefly—outlining on the board only the main ideas—or you may wish to work through each detail explaining the points as Dr. Harris does in his book. Be sure to stress that *all three psychological persons* are me and all are operative in me now. Also make sure that the students do not get the idea that the child is "bad," or the adult "good." We need all of them to be happy, healthy persons. If any is lacking or repressed, we become lopsided persons.

D. Which of the three persons is likely to dominate in you in the following situations:

—You come home from school and your mom is crabby because she has had a headache all day.
—You're babysitting and the kids won't go to bed.
—You're watching TV and your little sister wants to watch a different channel.
—You're caught cheating on a test.
—Your dad asks you to rake the lawn.
—A group of underclassmen comes into the lunchroom.
—You're bombing around in a car with a bunch of friends at 1:30 a.m.
—You lose a football game.
—You win the football championship game.
—You're fishing on a beautiful Saturday morning.
—You know you're going to be home a half hour later than you're expected.
—You sink into a tub full of warm water after a day of skiing.

E. Ask the class to draw a circle and divide it into three parts to show what share of an average day is dominated by each of the three persons.

Session 2 — PCA continued

A. Ask the students to list five things they remember their parents teaching them to do or not to do. Make a composite list on the board. It should include things like: take a bath, use clean language, share your candy, don't wet your pants, use a handkerchief, use good table manners, behave in school, say your prayers, do your homework, don't steal, keep out of fights, don't tell lies, watch out for cars, go to church every Sunday.

B. Remind the class that

> the child does what it feels like doing;
> the parent does what it's told—or makes someone else do so;
> the adult does what is reasonable and considerate.

For each of the things listed on the board, have the students write a number to show if they

   1. Still obey the parent. Do it "or else." I feel I "have to" do this thing.
   2. Disobey the parent. Give in to the child. I do what I feel like doing.
   3. Do the thing because I'm convinced it is the right thing to do. It has become part of my adult.
   4. Don't do it because I am convinced it is no longer necessary. This is also part of the adult.

C. Point out that it is hard to know sometimes whether a certain action is one or three, two or four. Rationalizing is a trick we are all good at—giving the adult fake reasons so that the child can have his way.

Session 3 — Six levels of morality[2]

A. Explain to the class that there are six levels of moral maturity—six reasons people have for doing the good things they do. Present the six, discussing each as you present it.

   1) Spanking level—this is doing the right thing to avoid some kind of physical punishment or some kind of discomfort. The prime motivator for the person on this level is fear.
   2) Lollipop level—this is doing the right thing to get some kind of reward or a good feeling. Discuss some of the lollipops that are offered throughout life to motivate people: grades, money, fringe benefits.
   3) Good boy (girl) level—this is doing the right thing in order to get approval. The persons whose approval we seek shift as we grow older—parents, teachers, friends, the neighbors, society, the boss.
   4) Play-by-the-rules level (law and order level)—this is doing the right thing because the rules of the game call for it—whether the "game" is poker, football, school, or life. The person motivated on this level believes in the rules (or laws) because he sees that the "game" doesn't work without them. He believes that he and everyone else should keep the law because law is a necessary part of life. Point out the difference between this and level one. He is not just afraid of being punished for breaking the law; he really believes the law should be obeyed.

[2]This is a modified version of the six stages of moral maturity as explained by Dr. Lawrence A. Kohlberg. A summary of Dr. Kohlberg's ideas can be found in Ronald Duska and Mariellen Whelan, *Moral Development: A Guide to Piaget and Kohlberg* (New York: Paulist Press, 1975).

5) Conviction level—this is doing the right thing because I am convinced it is right. Sometimes it might mean going against the law. If so, I am willing to take the consequences for doing so. I will do the thing I believe in regardless: if no one is watching me, if no one is going to reward me, if no one else is doing it. It is sometimes difficult to tell this from level two; in level two I do what feels right; here I do what I am convinced is right.

6) Love level[3]—this is doing the right thing out of love for someone. Have the students point out the difference between this and level three.

B. Point out the correlation between Kohlberg's stages and Parent-Child-Adult stages. Levels one and two roughly correspond to the child; levels three and four to the parent; and levels five and six to the adult.

C. Break up into small groups to discuss the following questions:

- What level are most people on at age 6? 10? 15? 18? 40?
- How free is a person who operates on each level? Where is the greatest freedom?
- How happy is a person who operates on each level? Why?
- What are the advantages and disadvantages of operating on each level?
- How do you deal with a person who is operating on each?
- On what level would you say Nixon was operating during the Watergate affair?

Session 4 — Levels of morality (cont.)

A. Duplicate and pass out papers like those on page 32. Explain: When we have to decide whether to do or not to do a certain good thing, various questions run through our minds. We don't necessarily allude to the questions, but they are there. They give us a clue as to what level we are acting on. Some of these questions are listed below. Read them to the class one by one. Ask the students to decide which level the question fits, and write it in the appropriate box on their sheets.

What will people say?	What's right is right.
What would make someone else happy?	Is there a law against it?
	What is the right thing to do?
Who's going to make me?	My parents say I have to.
What'll I get out of it?	What'll you pay me?
What should I do?	Who else is doing it?
What would Jesus do?	It's my job and I'll do it.
What'll happen if I don't?	Someone needs me.
How will it look?	We always do it that way.
How would I like to be treated?	I owe it to someone.
Do I have to?	Who'll know if I don't?
What's in it for me?	Someone has to do it, so I will.
How can I help someone?	What can I do to help?
Everybody else is doing it.	For you, anything!

B. Judging from the questions, on what level do you operate most often? Can you think of three things you did on each level during the last week or so?

[3]Love is used here in the highest Christian sense. It is completely other-centered and universal. Kohlberg himself does not use the word "love" to characterize this highest level of moral maturity. He explains it, rather, in terms of Kant's categorical imperative.

Session 5

A. Duplicate and pass out papers like the sample on p. 33. (Or use the questions given there orally as the basis for oral discussion of each question.) Explain: It isn't enough in life simply to avoid doing evil, we also have to do good, and we should do good for good reasons. For each of the 20 things listed, first decide if you would do the thing or not and write Yes or No in the last column. Then go back and decide on what level you would have made your decision.

B. When the students have completed these papers, use them for discussion. Be sure to honor the students' right to pass.

Session 6 — On internalizing our parents' values

A. We were all taught from childhood not to lie, not to steal, not to cheat. Have you internalized these values or not? Answer these questions honestly:

Where do you stand on lying?
  1. Under no circumstances. I believe in always telling the truth.
  2. Only to help someone else.
  3. Only as a last resort—no other way out.
  4. Only if I'm sure I won't get caught.
  5. Everybody does it—it can't be that bad.
  6. It's my way of life—I do it all the time.
Where do you stand on stealing?
Where do you stand on cheating?

B. It might be too threatening to share the results of this little exercise, but it should serve as a basis for a good discussion. Include in your discussion such questions as:

  • Do you believe in a double standard—one set of rules for yourself and another for the rest of the world?
  • How has Watergate affected your values in this line?
  • Do you expect people, especially parents, to trust you even though you lie to them?

1. Spanking level - to avoid punishment

2. Lollipop level - to get a reward

3. Good boy (girl) level - to get approval (of parents, friends, society)

4. Play-by-the-rules level - to keep the rules (of life, of the family, of the country)

5. Conviction level - to do the right thing

6. Love level - to help someone in need, out of unselfish concern for all others.

On what level would you decide?
Would you do the good thing?

You have to decide if you will . . .

	On what level would you decide?	Would you do the good thing?
1. steal $10.00 left on a teacher's desk		
2. tell your parents the truth about a fender dented while leaving a beer party		
3. speak respectfully to parents scolding you about your brother's mistake		
4. go to school when you feel like faking sick		
5. give your brother a birthday present — he didn't give you one		
6. give money to the missions		
7. go to classes — three good friends are skipping and want you to come		
8. not cheat on a math test — you're sitting next to the class brain		
9. go to Mass on Sunday and participate when you get there		
10. make your bed and clean your room		
11. do your assignments neatly		
12. talk to an unpopular student in the cafeteria		
13. stick up for an unpopular teacher when the other students are cutting him (her) down		
14. listen respectfully to your parents' explanation of the way things were "back then"		
15. report a serious act of vandalism		
16. not go to a party — you know if you go you'll get bombed		
17. quit drinking completely or cut down to one or two beers		
18. help a teacher carry some things or set up the gym		
19. attend a prayer meeting		
20. go to daily Mass		

(To make copies of this page, use duplicate in tear-out section at back of book.)

Three psychological persons can be found within each person:[4]

The Psychological Parent

1. Represents the *taught* concepts in life.

2. The psychological parent:
   pressures
   blames
   finds fault
   gives orders
   domineers

3. The parent is:
   strict
   uncompromising
   inconsistent
   protective

4. In the psychological parent are found:
   laws
   regulations
   sanctions
   prejudices
   taboos
   threats
   social pressures

5. In regard to others the parent:
   protects (overly)
   dominates
   blames
   finds fault

6. Sources of the parent are:
   parents
   teachers
   older children
   TV

The Psychological Adult

1. Represents the *thought* concepts.

2. The psychological adult:
   figures things out
   solves problems
   weighs consequences
   understands
   thinks things through

3. The adult is:
   aware
   creative
   responsible
   thoughtful

4. In the psychological adult are found:
   values
   ideas
   realities
   truths

5. In regard to others the adult:
   understands
   trusts
   loves

6. Sources of the adult are:
   experience
   examined data from the parent or the child

The Psychological Child

1. Represents the *felt* concepts.

2. The psychological child:
   plays
   pouts
   laughs
   cries
   explores

3. The child is:
   spontaneous
   curious
   charming
   playful
   demanding
   jealous
   carefree
   pouty

4. In the psychological child are found:
   wishes
   fears
   feelings
   guilts
   delights
   frustrations

5. In regard to others the child:
   enjoys
   uses
   manipulates
   takes advantage of

6. Sources of the child are:
   felt reactions to people, and experiences

[4]Adapted from *I'm OK, You're OK.*

(To make copies of this page, use duplicate in tear-out section at back of book.)

Unit 3

Sacraments/What They Are. What They Are To Me

The purpose of this unit is to help teens clarify the meaning of sacrament and the role the sacraments play in their life with God. In the unit a sacrament is defined as: a symbolic action that externalizes an experience of God and that deepens and intensifies the experience.[1]

The lessons in this unit presuppose that the sessions in Unit 1 on the experience of God have already been covered. If that is not the case, incorporate those lessons into this unit, after Session 3.

Session 1 is an exploratory lesson in which the teacher attempts to discover what the students know and how they feel about sacraments. Sessions 2 and 3 explain the concept of *symbolic action* as an important aspect of all human life. The remaining sessions explore the special symbolic actions the church calls sacraments, showing how these community actions externalize one's experience of God, and how they deepen the experience by externalizing it.

Session 1 — Sacrament defined

A. Have students write in their own words a definition of "sacrament." Share responses.

B. Write on the board the Baltimore Catechism definition: A sacrament is an outward sign instituted by Christ to give grace. (You will have to explain what the Baltimore Catechism is. They will be interested in hearing about how religion was taught to their parents.)

C. Have them list the seven sacraments as a kind of "fun" quiz. See how many can get all seven with the right names and spellings.

[1]For the theological foundations of this approach to sacraments see: Karl Rahner, *Theological Investigations XIV* (New York: Seabury, 1976), pp. 135–184.

D. Present the definition of sacraments we will be working with:

> A sacrament is a symbolic action
> that externalizes an experience of God
> and that deepens and intensifies the experience.

Give them a few minutes to begin memorizing this definition. Explain that you expect them to be able to write it from memory and explain it in some future test. In the meantime you will help them to understand each part of it.

E. Ask students to complete these statements:

> I was always taught that the sacraments...
> Now I don't understand...

Discuss responses. Don't try to resolve the problems brought out in this exercise, just try to get a clear picture of the problems for yourself and for the class. Indicate that the lessons coming up should help to resolve some of the problems.

Session 2 — Symbolic actions

A. See if someone can give you the definition of a sacrament taught in the last session. Write it on the board again and circle *symbolic action*.

B. Ask if anyone is wearing someone else's ring. Use this as an example to explain the definition of sacraments.

> Wearing the ring is a symbolic action.
> What experience does it *externalize*? (The experience of love and friendship.)
> How does wearing the ring *deepen* and *intensify* the experience of love?

Pick one of the "characters" in the class to use for the next example. Make up a little story something like: Frank comes to class in a crabby mood and throws his books down on the desk. What he doesn't realize until too late is that the teacher is also in a crabby mood. She yells at him to pick up the books and put them down quietly. Then she turns to write something at the board and when her back is turned, Frank makes a face at her. (If you're a good ham, do it up well!)

> What are the symbolic actions in this little scene? (Making a face and throwing the books.)
> What experience does it externalize? (Anger)
> How does it deepen the experience of anger?

C. Discuss: Why do we *want* to externalize our inner experiences?
   Why does Mary want to wear Fred's ring?
   Why did Frank want to make a face at me?
   Why do we want to give a gift to someone we love?

D. Write or work out in small groups: List five symbolic actions. Tell what each externalizes and how it deepens the experience externalized. (Some possibilities: handshake, kiss, punch, cheering at a game, giving candy after a fight.)

E. Some symbolic actions are formal and public affairs, eg. Inauguration of the President, Awards Assembly, Crowning of the Prom Queen. Discuss why these are done so formally.

As an example of the value of a public symbolic action, pick a student you know smokes too much. Say to her: "Wendy, you decide to quit smoking. You really make up your mind that the habit is stupid and expensive and ruining your singing voice, so you decide to quit. How effective will your decision be?" (After she has answered that she has tried than ten times already, go on.) "Since private resolutions don't work for you, you ask the principal if you can have three minutes of the next school assembly. On the assembly date you take a pack of cigarettes, stand on the stage in front of the whole school, and grind the pack into the floor with your heal. You tell the kids that you want to quit smoking and they should please help you to do it. How does this public symbolic action deepen your decision? Do you really think you could do something like that?"

F. Now apply the symbolic action idea to sacraments. What does the definition mean? Drill the definition again.

Session 3

A. Share lists made in D above. Use them as a way of repeating the sacrament definition several more times.

B. Give an example parallel to the smoking example above: You decide that you really want to live your Christian life the way Christ wants you to. You are going to spend time with God regularly, to give service to his people, to try to live up to his way of love. To reinforce that decision, you stand up in the church on a Sunday morning and publicly, before the whole congregation, announce your decision and ask for help in carrying it out. Supposing you really had the courage to do something like that. How would it deepen and intensify your commitment to Christianity?

Next, help the class to see that that was the kind of experience their confirmation should be or should have been. Was It? Will it be?

C. Explain: If sacraments are to be effective in our lives we must have:
   First: the experience of God
   Second: the symbolic action that externalizes the experience
   Third: the deepened experience (This third reality rarely happens if the first is missing.)
Discuss this in terms of the students' reception of the sacraments. What experience of God ought to precede the reception of each sacrament? (This will be answered more fully as we study each sacrament, but the class may get into a good discussion of what it takes to be really prepared for each sacrament.)

Session 4

A. Tell the class you will dictate to them a list of things. They are to indicate how important each thing is in their life by a number: 1—not important; 2—somewhat important; 3—very important. After they have written their answer call on the class to show everyone what they wrote by holding up the appropriate number of fingers.

sports	driver's license	skiing
school	hunting	girls (or guys)
grades	music	
clothes	family	
parties	spending money	

B. Using the same scheme, have them indicate how important they think baptism, confirmation, eucharist, penance are. Do each sacrament separately, and chart the responses on the board—i.e., tell how many ones, twos or threes for each. Call on various students to explain why they used the number they did. Ask such questions as:

- Do you think it's significant that skiing is more important to you than sacraments?
- Do you think the sacraments could mean more to you than they do?
- What could make that happen?

Session 5 — Symbolic actions in a love relationship

A. Tell the story of Jack and Carlita (If there are students by those names in your class, change the names.)

(It is up to the teacher to tell this story in such a way that you bring it to life. Do not give the students this to read. It is just the bare outlines of a story plot which it is up to you to bring to life.)

Jack and Carlita live in Chicago, only a few blocks from one another but in very different neighborhoods. Carlita was born to a 16-year-old girl who didn't want her. She lived in a sort of tenement house where no one really bothered about her much except to see that she got some kind of food and something to wear. When she got to school, she was tough, knew how to fight for what she wanted. When she reached her teen years Carlita discovered something about herself—she was beautiful. And she quickly learned how to use her beautiful body to get the kind of attention she had been missing all her life.

Jack grew up in a good Christian home, with lots of love and attention. He was a good kid and a good student, popular and fun to have around. One thing about Jack that was special was his interest in people. He always wanted to know what made people tick—why they did the things they did, why they thought the way they did about things.

One Friday night Jack and his friends decide to "invade" the dance at the neighborhood public school which Carlita attends. In the course of the evening Jack sees Carlita, likes what he sees, and asks her for a dance. He spends some time with her, but when he gets back to his friends they begin to tease him. They've been checking out Carlita's reputation and tell Jack that they're quite sure she's not his kind of girl.

Jack is puzzled. The girl he met doesn't seem to fit the reputation the boys have described. True to his nature, Jack decides to find out for himself more about this girl and what makes her the way she is.

Carlita, in the meantime, can't figure Jack out, either. Here is a guy who is obviously interested in her, and obviously not in the way most of the boys she knows have been interested.

When the evening is over, Jack has Carlita's phone number in his pocket. And in the weeks and months that follow, the two young people see much of each other. Carlita becomes a new person. She gets rid of her old rough ways, and discovers within herself all kinds of new and beautiful things she never knew existed. To make a long story short—Jack marries Carlita and they live happily ever after.

B. Explain to the students that the story above is actually a parody of a story found in the Old Testament. If you have a mature class you may want them to read it: Ezekiel 16:1–16.[2] The story there is much cruder, much more realistic and earthy than this version, but the lesson is the same: Jack in the story represents God, Carlita represents us. Draw out the following points of comparison:

- God comes into my life first. He comes looking for me. He starts the relationship.
- He loves me the way I am, and if I accept his presence, he can come to me many times in many ways.
- God's love in my life changes me. It brings out the best in me. It puts into me new and beautiful qualities.
- This presence of God in my life is what the church has traditionally called grace.
- Grace can be defined as: "God-loving-me-loving-God-loving-me...."

C. Have the class point out some of the symbolic actions that would have characterized the growing relationship between Jack and Carlita. (Smiles, kisses, holding hands, meeting at the drugstore, eating at each other's home, exchanging class rings, making up after a fight.)

D. Three essential elements of a love relationship:
   1. Time spent together.
   2. Special, one-time-only symbolic actions. These are performed once but the effects last for a long time. In a love relationship the most frequent symbol used is the exchange of rings—class rings, engagement rings, wedding rings. Each of these symbols indicates a basic change in the relationship.
   3. Daily, oft-repeated symbolic actions. These are done over and over, and in a real love relationship, always with new and deeper meaning. E.g.: kisses, eating together, and forgiving.

Draw the comparison between this and the developing relationship with God. If that relationship is to develop we must have the same three elements:
   1. Time spent with God—prayer. There can be no real relationship with God without this. Sacraments are meaningless symbols unless we have prepared for them by spending time getting close to God. Help the teens to see that this would be like exchanging rings with someone they did not even know.
   2. Special, one-time-only symbolic actions that alter our relationship with God, put it on a new level. Baptism, confirmation, and orders are this kind of symbolic action. In a sense matrimony would fit here also. It is not a "character" sacrament like the others, but it does bring us before God in an entirely new capacity.
   3. Daily, oft-repeated symbolic actions. The obvious sacraments here are eucharist and penance. Anointing of the sick fits too, but with a bit of difficulty.

E. Both the God-experience and the symbolic actions that externalize it are part of an on-going relationship of love between God and me. Several things should be remembered here—

[2]This application of the Ezekiel passage to the life of grace is adapted from a similar story told by Piet Fransen in *The New Life of Grace,* (New York: Herder and Herder, 1972).

1) God starts the relationship. He loves me first, gives himself to me first, calls me to be his friend. So the experience of God depends *first* on God.

2) The official symbolic actions that externalize the God-experience (the sacraments) also come from God, through Christ and the church.

3) When I celebrate a sacrament, I am participating with Christ (and the rest of the church) in a symbolic action that externalizes both Christ's love for me and my love for him (as well as the love of the church members for one another).

4) The deepening of the God-experience depends partly on Christ and partly on me. Christ is always present in the celebration of the sacrament, offering me his love and grace. I might be really "present" there to accept and return his love, and I might just be going through the motions.

Session 6

A. By this time the students will probably have raised the objection that Baptism for them was not the first step in their relationship with God, that it was done for them when they were infants and they had no say in the matter. To clarify this matter, explain to the students the difference between the way marriages are arranged now and the way they were arranged in the middle ages.

- Back then the parents arranged for the marriage, sometimes when the children were still very small. You grew up knowing that someday you would be the husband or wife of the princess or prince in the next castle. When the two young people reached marriage age they ratified (or broke as it happens in all the stories) the agreement their parents had made for them.

- Baptism for us is like marriage in the middle ages. When we are children, our parents promise for us that we will grow up in a loving relationship with God. And when we are old enough we *confirm* (or reject as the case may be) the commitment made by our parents.

B. Ask the students which arrangement they think would be better—baptism at infancy or waiting until adulthood when the person can make his or her own decision. (This question will be explored more fully in the unit on baptism and confirmation. At that time a full-scale debate will be held on the question of infant baptism.)

Session 7

A. The three yeses

Explain to the students that a developing love relationship needs three yeses. (Use as an example one of the boys who won't be embarrassed.)

Mark here has his eye on one of the sophomore girls. She is in his history class but she always sits in the front with her friends. Mark has been wishing for weeks that she would notice him, but as far as she's concerned, Mark doesn't even exist. If this relationship is going to get off the ground, Sue has to say three yeses:

Yes, Mark, you exist.

Yes, Mark, you like me.

Yes, I like you, too.

These same three yeses are necessary in the relationship with God. He has had his eye on you for 15 or 16 years, but the relationship can't get far unless you can say:

Yes, God, you exist. You really are.

Yes, God, you love me.

Yes, God, I love you, too.

See if the students can see in these the three theological virtues: faith, hope, and charity. If they've never heard of them, don't push it.

Ask the students what advice they would give to Mark with his problem of getting Sue to notice him. And what advice would they give to God in his big problem of getting them to notice him?

B. Using the open question technique,[3] ask each individual to tell which of the three yeses he thinks he is already saying to God, and to explain his answer.

Session 8 — Candles and sacraments (This lesson could also be used after all of the units on the individual sacraments have been completed.)

A. Gather in a setting where the students can sit in a circle comfortably. Have a taper candle for each student, and for yourself a larger candle to represent Christ, a tiny candle with the wick cut short, and several other tapers. If possible darken the room.

B. Begin by discussing darkness—what it means to them, what it has always meant to humanity.

Then light the Christ candle. Discuss why it is that humanity has always used fire as a symbol of God. What are the things about fire that remind people of God? Next discuss the small candle. What are the things that make a candle a good symbol of humanity?

C. Explain that the candle's whole purpose for being is to be lighted. It doesn't matter how beautiful or how grubby it looks, if it lights, it's good; if it doesn't, it's not good. What does this have to say about humans and God? Discuss what it costs the candle to be lighted, what the candle has to do to keep burning, for whom the candle burns, how the flame is passed from one candle to another. With each question, of course, draw the parallel with the God-human relationship.

Define a Christian as a person who carries in his life the fire of God's love and who shares that fire wherever he goes.

D. Help the students explain each sacrament in candle terminology:

Baptism (adult): This is the decision a person makes to accept the life of God. Discuss what it will cost, why a person would choose to be "lit" when it will cost so much. (He has to constantly give himself to the fire or it will go out.) At this time the fire from the Christ candle could be used to light the students' candles. Further discussion could center on things like: there is really only one fire in the room—we all received part of the life of Christ at baptism; anyone can pass on the fire of God's love, not just a priest; you can't just walk up and "light" another person's candle, you have to first "warm" him by love and good example.

[3]Values Clarification, p. 139 ff.

Baptism (infant): Explain that most of us were baptized as infants. Use the very small candle. If you have cut the wick short enough, it will light, but the least flick of your wrist will put it out. Help the students to see that a baby baptized cannot keep his fire going; it must be nourished in a Christian family (use two candles, burning, to represent the family and put the tiny new flame into their joint flame.)

Confirmation: For those baptized as infants, confirmation is the celebration of the young person's decision to live his Christianity apart from the family's protective circle. The Bishop comes to give us the special power we will need to keep that flame going without our parents' help. (The proper age for confirmation might be discussed briefly.)

Matrimony: When two candles are joined, the double flame burns much brighter. When a Christian man and woman give themselves to one another in love, the life of God grows within them. The sacrament of marriage is repeated in each act of love—in each act God's grace grows. (This point will be a totally new idea for most of your students and may need more explanation. The sex act itself is sacramental when performed by married Christians).

Orders: Choose a taller candle to represent a priest. A priest in candle terminology is one whose whole life is dedicated to keeping candles burning brightly. Discuss what kind of person you would need for such a role; how he would be treated by the rest; the need for him to spend much time with God keeping his own flame burning.

Anointing of the sick: Take a battered candle and break it in several places. Discuss the role of prayer in the life of the sick; what it means to the sick person to have the priest and his family gather to pray with him and for him. Emphasize that this sacrament is for the sick not just the dying, and often the power of prayer heals the sick person. Discuss death in terms of candle. Death is not when the fire goes out; it is when the entire candle is caught up in the fire of God's eternal love.

Penance: Discuss the meaning of sin as a decision to put out the fire of God in our lives (serious sin) or a reducing of the intensity of the flame (lesser sin). Point out the need for someone else to relight our flame if it has gone out altogether.

Eucharist: Eucharist is the celebration of our Christianity. With the priest we gather around Christ, the source of our light. (Have several students put their flames together in the Christ flame.) This helps us to keep our own fire burning brightly. After Mass we are more ready to carry the life and love of Christ into our corner of the world.

Unit 4

Baptism and Confirmation/Membership in the Catholic Church

Because baptism and confirmation are sacraments of initiation,[1] this unit approaches these two sacraments from the viewpoint of membership in the Catholic Church. The aim of the unit is to help the teens to understand what it means to be a Catholic Christian, and to encourage them to examine the degree of personal commitment they have already made to Catholicism. Hopefully the unit will bring the teens closer to making an adult decision to commit their lives to Christ and to his church.

Although aware of the current debate in theological circles concerning the historical meaning of confirmation and the separation of the sacraments of initiation,[2] the author has opted to develop these lessons on the current pastoral understanding of Confirmation as a sacrament of mature commitment to Christianity. This seems to be the only viable option open to catechists at the present time, since we are dealing with groups of adolescents nearly all of whom were baptized as infants. A young person should not be confirmed until he or she is mature enough to make a decision for Christianity, a decision which is not unduly influenced by parental wishes or pressures.

From the viewpoint of the adolescent, the important aspect of these sacraments is commitment to Christ and membership in the church. The theological debate is discussed with them in terms of that commitment.

Session 1 — What is a Catholic Christian?

A. Divide the class into groups of three or four. Give each group a large sheet of paper and a marker. Have them divide the paper into two columns. In the first they should write: *A Christian is a person who . . .* and list as many items as they can that would identify a Christian. When the groups have exhausted their ideas, give them the heading for the second column: *A Catholic is a person who. . . .* In this column they should list only those things that differentiate Catholics from other Christians. (They will find this more difficult.)

B. Hang up the sheets and compare them.

C. Pass out duplicates of the form on page 44. Compare student lists to these. Ask students to grade themselves as Catholics and as Christians, using the grading system in the right-hand corner of the form. Discuss.

[1]Eucharist, the third sacrament of initiation is discussed in the following unit.
[2]For an overview of this debate, see *Made Not Born* (Notre Dame University Press, 1976) as well as articles found in *Worship* and *Living Light*.

What is a Christian?   D-Definitely   S-Somewhat
                                            T-Trying   N-Not really

A Christian is a person who

_____believes in God

_____believes in the Blessed Trinity

_____believes that Jesus Christ is God

_____believes that Jesus died for human beings and rose again

_____believes that Jesus lives now in our midst

_____accepts Jesus as a personal friend and savior

_____prays to the Father as Jesus taught

_____keeps the ten commandments and Jesus' commandments of love

_____tries to live according to the teachings of Jesus:

—to love God above all

—to love others as ourselves

—to forgive our enemies

—to care for the poor and lowly

—to treat all people as brothers and sisters

What is a Catholic Christian?

A Catholic Christian is one who, *besides* the things listed above:

_____accepts the Pope as Christ's representative on earth

_____celebrates the eucharist every Sunday with other Catholics

_____believes that Jesus is present in the eucharist

_____receives Holy Communion during the Easter time

_____confesses at least once a year

_____contributes to the support of the church

_____believes that the best way to live the Christian life is within the Catholic Church

_____receives the sacraments within the Catholic Church

(To make copies of this page, use duplicate in tear-out section at back of book.)

Session 2

A. Discuss these two questions: Can you be a Catholic without being a Christian? Can you be a Christian without being a Catholic?

B. Explain the place of Catholicism in the total picture of world religions. Present the timeline below, showing the beginnings of the great religions of the world.

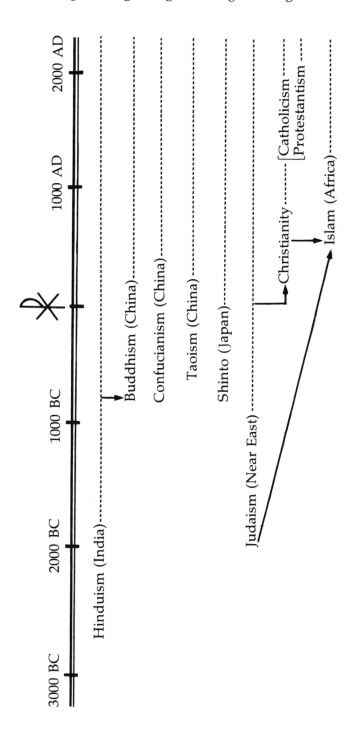

Indicate on the time line the great religions of the world. Point out that Christianity is an offshoot of Judaism. (Jesus was a Jew who claimed to fulfill the Jewish expectations for a Messiah.) Explain the Reformation in the 16th Century when Christianity was split. All those who disagreed with the Catholic position came to be known as Protestants. These include Lutherans, Presbyterians, Methodists, Episcopalians, etc.

D. Assignment: Give the students the question "Why be a *Catholic* Christian?" Have them list at least five reasons why a person would want to be a member of the Catholic church.

Session 3 — Why be a Catholic?

A. Using the homework assignment, make a composite list on the board of all the reasons why a person might be a Catholic. List both "good" reasons and "bad" reasons. When the list is complete, ask the students to place a + sign next to what they consider good reasons, and a − sign next to what they consider bad reasons for belonging to the church. Next ask them to pick out the three reasons on the board that best answer the question for themselves: Why are *you* a Catholic?

B. Interview individual students in the class.[3]
Some possible questions are given here:

- Do you think you will be a practicing Catholic 10 years from now?
- Do you want to be married in the Catholic Church? Do you want the blessing of the church on your marriage, or do you just want to use the building for the ceremony?
- Will you be a supporting member of the church? How much will you give?
- Do you think you'll ever give some years—or your whole life—to the service of the church?
- Will you be the kind of Catholic who can be called on to be a lector, usher, permanent deacon, choir member, CCD teacher?
- Will you send your children to a Catholic grade school? high school?
- If you had not been baptized as a baby, would you want to be baptized now?
- Have you ever been sorry that your parents raised you Catholic?
- What services do you expect from your pastor?
- How do you think the church should go about getting the money it needs to carry on its work?

[3] *Values Clarification*, p. 139.

Session 4 — Adult baptism

A. To understand adult baptism, refer back to the earliest days of the church when the baptism of adults was the common practice. Review the definition of a sacrament learned earlier: A sacrament is a symbolic action that externalizes an experience of God and that deepens and intensifies the experience.

What was the *experience of God* that led a person to seek baptism in the early church? (The person had come in contact with a community of Christians whose lives showed that they were close to God, that they loved one another, that they believed that Jesus had died and risen from the dead. The person was convinced that God loved him, also, in a special way, and that God wanted him to be a part of this group of people who called themselves Christians. He was willing to live the style of life they lived, and to give up anything in his life that was contrary to that way of life.)

Once the young man or woman had made a decision, he or she was ready to go through the *symbolic action* of baptism. This included:

- 40 days of prayer and instruction in the faith (This is where our present practice of Lent originated.)
- An all-night prayer vigil on Holy Saturday night. The baptism took place that night. Ask the students why.
- Questioning by the bishop or priest to see if the candidate was really ready for baptism and knew what he was getting into.
- The baptismal promises. A public promise to give up Satan and all his evil ways.
- The candidate stripped off all his clothes as a sign that he was giving up his old way of life.
- He went down into the water. Usually he was completely immersed. The celebrant pronounced the words of baptism: I baptize....
- When he came out of the water his body was anointed with oil, and those present prayed that he would be filled with the Holy Spirit. (It is this part of the ceremony that is now called confirmation.)
- He was given a new white garment, as a sign of the new life in Christ that was now his.
- He was given a candle, lighted from the Easter candle, as a sign that he was now filled with the light of Christ.
- He was led in procession to the church where the Easter Mass was celebrated and he received his first communion.

B. Direct questions such as these to individuals in the class:

1) What do you think about this complex kind of symbolic action?
2) If you weren't a Christian now, would you go through such a set of symbols to become one?
3) What part of the ceremony would you find frightening? difficult? exciting?
4) Can you think of any experience in your world that compares to this?
5) Should the church return to this kind of rich symbolic action?
6) Explain how this total experience would lead to the *deepened experience* of one's Christian faith.

Session 5 — Infant Baptism

A. Probably everyone in your class was baptized as an infant. Explain that infant baptism is in response to a religious experience of the <u>parents</u>.

What was the experience of God that prompted your parents to have you baptized? (They were members of a church that brought them close to God. They wanted their child also to be a member of that Christian family. They made a decision to raise you as a Christian, to teach you, from little on, who God was and what he expected of you as a person.)

Your parents brought you to the church for the public symbolic action of baptism. (Have the class point out the remnants of the original baptismal ceremony that can still be found in today's baptism.) They officially enrolled you in the Catholic church, and promised in your name that you would grow up in the faith.

How will this public symbolic action deepen and intensify the parents' decision to raise you as a Catholic?

B. In most cases, when the child is baptized as an infant, he confirms his baptism as a young adult. This is his chance to ratify publicly the commitment made in his name by his parents and godparents at baptism.

C. *Assignment:* Explain to the class that there has been a long debate among various Christian churches concerning the best age for baptism (and confirmation). Some churches, including the Catholic Church, believe in baptizing infants; some believe that only adults should be baptized. (The Catholic Church prescribes the baptism of infants in Canon 770.) Ask the class to write three reasons in favor of each of the following:

   1) Baptizing infants
   2) Putting off baptism until adulthood, when the person is old enough to choose for himself.
   3) Confirming children in seventh or eighth grade.
   4) Putting off confirmation till young adulthood—age 18 or over.

Session 6 — Baptism takes away original sin

A. Write across the top of the board in large letters, THE WORLD IS A MESS. Ask the students to write all over the board words and phrases to prove that statement, e.g., drunkenness, cheating, Watergate, war. (Or the class can call out the words for the teacher to write on the board.)

B. When the board is pretty well filled, place a little stick-man someplace in the middle of the mess. Ask the class: This child was just born into the world. What effect will the mess have on his life? To what extent does the evil in the world get inside of him? Can a child ever escape the effects of the evil in the world altogether? Explain that another name for the mess in the world that affects every person coming into the world is original sin. Point out that original doesn't mean first—it means having to do with our *origins*.

C. Ask: If this is what original sin means, what does it mean to say that baptism takes away original sin? What does it *not* mean? Discuss these questions, then offer this explanation:

- If original sin is understood as the power of evil permeating our lives, then we can see that a ceremony in church can't just wash it away. Baptism is not magic. It is not automatic.

- How might God protect that little child from all that evil in the world? Help students see that God works through a community of people. Diagram around the child a circle of people, all of whom are dedicated to resisting evil, to overcoming it, to keeping it out of their own lives and the lives of their children. What is such a group called? (The church.) What is the relationship between the church and baptism?

  Offer this answer:

- *Adult baptism* is a decision to resist evil and to let God's power over evil work in my life. It is a decision to join a Christian community which has pledged to let its members' lives be governed by the power of God's love rather than by the power of evil.

- *Infant baptism* is the parents' decision to enroll their child in the community of those whose lives have been touched by Christ. (Place a ⚓ in the circle of people surrounding the child to indicate that Christ is present in his life through them.) Through baptism the child becomes part of the Christian community. Christ himself lives in the heart of the baptized child and works through the daily lives of these Christian people to protect the growing child from evil, and to help the child grow in truth and honesty, justice and love until the day that he is old enough to choose (or reject) the way of God's love over the way of evil.

D. Written assignment: "Baptism takes away original sin": Write an essay telling what that doesn't mean, what it does mean.

Session 7

A. Explain: Refer again to the "mess" the world is in. People respond to the mess in the world in various ways. Draw little stick-men scattered over the board. Give each a little cartoon "balloon" in which you print his response to the mess in the world. As you write each on the board, have the class discuss how a person who gives that response would act.

- "Get what you can." (This is the Archie Bunker response. Take care of old number one. Forget about the rest of the mess.)
- "Make stricter laws." (Control the mess by making laws. Punish anyone who steps out of line.)
- "Who cares?" (As long as I get what I want, the mess doesn't bother me.)
- "Let George do it." (Somebody ought to do something about the mess the world is in. Who, me? Well, I really don't have time.)

- "I'll try." (I can help. I can't do it all, but I'm willing to do my part to make this a better world.)
- "Build a wall." (Build a perfect city, or nation, or club. Let only the "right" people in. Seal off the mess.)
- "I'd help, but. . . ." (Have the students give various things that might follow the "but.")
- "If you can't beat 'em, join 'em." (Everybody else is doing it, so it can't be that bad.)
- "Love is the answer." (If everyone would work at loving and respecting everyone else, the mess would gradually go away.)

D. Ask: What is the Christian response to the mess in the world? (The class will see it in the last answer.) Point out that the kind of love that will overcome the power of evil in the world is a very special kind of love. Jesus came to teach us about this kind of love—the love God has for man, the love Jesus had for the world. "By this will men know that you are my disciples, that you love one another *as I have loved you*." "The measure of love is that you are willing to lay down your life for another." It takes the power of God's love to overcome the world's mess, and we find that love in a community of persons who try to live the Christian life, the church.

F. Ask students: Which answer to the world's mess do you think is given most frequently by the people you know? Which answer do you give? How many people do you know who really give the Christian answer?

Session 8 — Confirmation

A. Bring an apple to class. Cut it open and take out one little seed. Ask the class to explain the difference between an apple seed and an apple tree. (The role of an apple seed is to *take in life*, to draw into itself soil and sun and water, and to grow. The role of the tree is to *give life*. It still takes in soil and sun and rain, but if it doesn't give any life back, we cut it down because it's no good.) Ask the class what the apple seed has to say about the difference between the child and the adult.

B. Confirmation is the sacrament of Christian adulthood. Look at confirmation in terms of the definition of a sacrament.

What *experience of God* would lead a young person to choose to be confirmed?

- He has lived the Christian faith for some time. He feels it brings him closer to God, helps him to be a better person.
- He wants to take his place as an adult in the church—not just a receiver who soaks in life, but a mature Christian who is ready to give life, to help the poor, the sick, the lonely.
- He knows and understands his faith well enough that he can explain it to others, especially his own future children.
- He loves his faith and wants to be a member of his church for the rest of his life.
- He is willing to profess his faith openly, to live up to it even if those around him don't, to defend it against attackers, if necessary.

What is the *symbolic action* that is a sign of his personal commitment to God and the church?

- He comes before a gathering of Christians and the official representative of God and the church—the bishop or his delegate.
- He proclaims publicly by his presence there that he is ready to take his place among the adult members of the church.
- The bishop questions him to see if he really does understand his faith and his responsibilities as an adult Christian.
- The bishop anoints him with oil as a sign of strength and prays that he be given the fullness of the Holy Spirit.
- The bishop shakes his hand or embraces him as a sign of welcome into the community of mature Christians. (That is what the former tap on the cheek was intended to symbolize. It has been replaced by the handshake because the tap was misunderstood by most people.)

How does this symbolic action *deepen and intensify* the young Christian's desire to really live his faith in a mature manner?

C. If students in your class have been confirmed, discuss with them the relationship between the ideal presented above and their experience of the sacrament.

Session 9 — Levels of commitment

Recall the six levels of morality discussed in unit two, and list them on the board. Explain: There are people in the church who have accepted their baptism and church membership on each of the six levels. Discuss:

What would be the main concern of a person whose religious commitment was on each level?

At what level of commitment would you say a person was ready for the symbolic action of confirmation? How would you judge a person's readiness?

At what level would you place most adult Catholics you know? How do you judge this?

At what level would you place yourself? your friends? How do you judge this? What could change it?

Answers to the first question above might be:

1. Spanking level (Main concern is avoiding the punishment of God in hell or the punishment of parents on earth.)
2. Lollipop level (Main concern is getting the reward of heaven or the reward of feeling good because I went to church.)
3. Good boy/girl level (Main concern is pleasing my parents, or looking good to the neighbors, doing what is expected of a good person, etc.)
4. Law and order (Main concern is keeping the laws of God and of the church because I believe in their importance.)
5. Conviction level (Main concern is doing what I think God expects of me—giving God what I really owe him.)
6. Love level (Main concern is love for God and the church. I accept baptism with great joy as a gift from a God who loves me.)

Note: If your students have been exposed to the Catholic Charismatic movement, they may wonder where what the charismatics call "baptism of the Holy Spirit" fits into this picture. In the scheme presented above, it seems that the realization of one's faith on the level of love is the experience that the charismatics would call "Baptism of the Spirit." It is important to point out that one does not have to attend prayer meetings or be prayed over in order to have that experience. It is a gift from God given to those who are faithful to him in prayer and service.

Session 10 — Debate on ideal age for baptism and confirmation

A. Select three students who are willing to argue in favor of infant baptism, and three who wish to argue for adult baptism. (The individual doesn't necessarily have to support the position he is debating for.) Set up a debate situation in front of the class. You serve as moderator to be sure everyone has a chance to talk and to keep the debate flowing smoothly. Encourage the debaters to support their arguments with reasons. Allow non-debaters to ask questions or present additional points at any time. If the debate lags, throw out a new problem like one of the following:

- You are a young priest. Your brother is married and has a new baby. You know that your brother and his wife never go to church anymore. They come to you and want you to baptize the baby. You ask them if that means they are promising to raise the child in the faith, to see that he learns his religion, and goes to church regularly. They have to admit that the baptism doesn't really mean that to them. They really want the baby baptized because that's what their parents expect them to do. Will you baptize the baby or won't you?

- You are the pastor of a large parish. You have to decide whether you will confirm all the seventh and eighth graders, or whether you will postpone confirmation until at least junior year in high school when students are old enough to decide for themselves. You know if you let them wait, they won't all be confirmed. Which would you prefer: 100 teens who were confirmed because the class was, or 30 who chose to be confirmed?

- It is 10 years from now and you have your first child. Will you have him baptized, or wait and let him choose? (Direct this question especially toward those who have been arguing for delaying baptism.)

- It is 25 years from now. You have a 16-year-old son who has not been confirmed. The pastor announces that confirmation classes will be starting next Monday for all the teens who feel they are ready to make a mature commitment to their faith. All the neighbors' kids are joining the confirmation class, but your son doesn't seem to be the least bit interested. What will you do? What would your parents do in this case?

B. If you do not have time to include the above points in the debate, they would make good material for another session. They could also be used for role playing.

C. Have the students write an essay in which they explain what decision they have come to regarding the best age for baptism and confirmation, and why.

Session 11 — Prayer service

As the closing session of this unit, plan a prayer service in which the students are given a chance to renew their baptismal promises. A sample prayer service is given below.

RENEWAL OF BAPTISM

I. "Remember this—I am with you always!"

Lighting of Christ candle.

Reading: Matt. 28: 16–20

II. "Unless a man is born again..."

Reading: John 3: 1–6, 16

Discussion

III. Renewal of baptism

a) Write a short promise something like this:
I, Mary Jones, promise God and my classmates that I will really try to live the Christian life. I will try to get to know Jesus better and to live his message.

b) Place your promise on the altar and receive a lighted candle as a symbol of your promise and of God's life in you.

IV. Pray the Our Father together

V. Reading: Romans 6: 1–14

VI. Of my hands I give to you, O Lord[4]
Of my hands I give to you.
I give to you as you gave to me
Of my hands I give to you.

Of my life ...

Of my self ...

Session 12 — Feedback

A. Conclude the unit with a feedback session. Write the following sentence starters on the board and give students time to write short answers to them. (Or assign them for homework and ask for paragraph-length answers.)

1) I am (glad, sorry) that my parents had me baptized as a baby because....
2) When I am a parent I (will, will not) have my children baptized as infants because....
3) The idea in this unit that most surprised me was....
4) I still don't understand....
5) I have definitely made up my mind to....

B. Using the open question technique,[5] discuss the answers with the class.

[4]F.E.L. Publications, Ltd. 1925 Pontius Avenue, Los Angeles, CA 90025.
[5]*Values Clarification*, pp. 139 and 158.

Unit 5

Eucharist[1]

The purpose of this unit is to bring the teens to a deeper understanding of the gift of eucharist, to value this sacrament as a central mystery of Christianity, and to participate joyfully and intelligently in its celebration.

Negative attitudes toward attendance at Sunday Mass are one of the most difficult problems the teacher of adolescents has to deal with. This unit attempts to face that problem head on by:

— giving the adolescents opportunities to look at their own attitudes and how these might have developed

— helping them to better understand what the eucharist could and should mean to them

— giving them opportunities to actually experience the eucharist as a loving gathering of Christians "in remembrance" of Jesus

— and, it is hoped, bringing them to a new appreciation of this sacrament in their own lives.

The teacher is encouraged to read through the entire unit carefully, including the scripture passages assigned in the various lessons, and to spend some time before teaching the unit prayerfully considering his or her own attitude toward eucharist.

Session 1 — Where we are

A. Explain to the class that the word "eucharist" applies to the Mass and communion. Have them complete in writing the statement: What I don't understand about eucharist (Mass, communion) is.... Complete the phrase with several statements if there are several things they don't understand. Go around the class sharing answers. Record these on a large sheet of newsprint for future reference. As one problem is given, ask for a show of hands of students who have a similar problem. Show the total on the paper.

B. Next, complete the statement: The best Mass I ever attended was.... As answers are shared, question the students as to why the Mass they mention was special.

[1]*Catechist*, November, 1978.

C. Ask the class when was the last time they were really taught something about eucharist. (For many it will have been in second grade.)

D. Have students write and complete the following statement:
If I were responsible for the Sunday Masses at our parish I would.... As students are sharing these answers, ask them if they are just complaining or if they would really be willing to do something about Sunday Masses—help to prepare for them, join a singing group, etc. Tell them you will call the pastor and volunteer their services if they want you to. (They will gasp!)

Session 2 — The eucharist as a farewell gift

A. To help the students to understand what kind of reality eucharist is, tell or read the following story.

Mike's Star

It was the opening week of school, and I was doing what I like best to do—getting to know a new group of teenagers. It was probably about the third day of class that I noticed Mike's star. I doubt if I would have paid attention to it at all if it hadn't been so out of place—a beautiful little silver lapel-tack, stuck conspicuously on the neck band of a worn-out sweatshirt! The next day I noticed the star again, this time pinned on the collar of Mike's faded flannel shirt. The third time I saw it, my curiosity got the best of me. "Hey, Mike," I asked after class. "What's with the star?" Mike smiled, "It's a long story, Sister. Got time for it?"

I had time, and here is Mike's story:

Mike's father had been a doctor, a highly respected neurologist. "I suppose you could even say he was famous," Mike said sheepishly. He was a very busy man, as doctors usually are, but he was, nonetheless, an exceptionally wonderful father to his six children. He believed in spending time with his family—real time, sharing time.

Mike was the oldest of the children, and the only boy. His special time to be with his dad was after dark, when the stars came out. Mike and his father would often go for long walks "out beyond the town where the stars really had a chance," Mike said. "Dad knew a lot about astronomy," he added. "I could name all the major constellations by the time I was 10."

But their conversations weren't only about stars. Mike was one of those lucky youngsters who could talk to his dad about anything. During those walks under the stars he learned all the beautiful and difficult things about life and the world and people that a boy needs to learn from his dad.

When Mike was in eighth grade, it was discovered that his father had cancer of the throat. "That's no way to go, Sister," Mike said, his face showing again some of the agony of that bitter year. It was a long and excruciating illness. The best remedies that medicine knew were tried. Some seemed to help for a time, but the disease progressed mercilessly nevertheless. Eventually it affected the vocal chords, and Mike's dad completely lost his power of speech.

"When Dad knew he had only a few weeks left to live, he asked to be brought home," Mike told me. "He wanted to spend his last days with Mom and us kids."

One night shortly after that, Mike's mother told Mike that his dad wanted to see him. Mike slipped quietly into the bedroom, pained by the sight of the emaciated man lying so feebly against the pillows. "Dad couldn't even smile," Mike said. "He just looked at me, steadily and gently, and all the love in the world was in his eyes. Then he took a tiny jewelry box off the bedstand and pressed in into my hand." Mike said he just kissed his dad and ran out of the room, crying. That night his father died.

In the box was the silver lapel-tack star. Mike told me he had worn that star every day since his father's death. Sometimes he'd forget it on yesterday's shirt and have to run down to the basement to dig it out of the wash. "This star keeps me going," Mike said, touching it fondly. "And it also keeps me out of trouble—most of the time," he laughed. "It just helps me to remember the kind of man Dad wanted me to be."

Mike graduated several years ago. He's in med school now, studying to be a neurologist like his father. But Mike and his star are still an important part of my life. His story, more than any theology I have ever studied, has helped me to understand, and to explain to my students, what the Eucharist is all about.

B. Ask the class to write in their notes five things that the star represented in Mike's life. List their answers on the board. Explain: The story about Mike is the best way I know of explaining to you what the eucharist is all about. The eucharist, too, is a gift that was given by someone who loved the night before he died. Everything the star meant to Mike tells us something about what Jesus wanted the eucharist to mean to his friends and followers.

Draw these comparisons from the class:

The eucharist is
- a symbol of Christ himself
- a means of keeping him present after death
- a symbol of all the times he had spent with his friends
- a summary of everything he taught, everything he stood for (Have the class recall several special events and special teachings in Jesus' life that were associated with bread and wine or with eating with his friends.)
- a sign of his deep love and of his friends' love for him
- a reminder to continue his work after death
- a source of strength against temptation

Session 3

A. Have the students work in small groups to develop answers to these questions. All should write answers in their notebooks as they work. Mike's father gave Mike a symbolic *thing*, a star; Jesus gave his church a symbolic *action*, eating bread and drinking wine together.

   1) Why did Jesus choose an action rather than a thing as his going-away symbol?
   2) Why the action of eating?
      (Eating is a natural sign of life, what we eat becomes a part of us, eating is a universal action, we usually eat with a family or people we love, everyone has to eat to live.)
   3) Why the eating of bread and the drinking of wine? Why not some other food and beverage?
      (Bread and wine are common food for common people; bread is a sign of work, wine a sign of joy; many of Jesus' great miracles had to do with bread and wine; much of his teaching was centered around bread and wheat, wine and grapes; both bread and wine are natural symbols of unity—small particles are ground together to make one loaf and one cup.)
   4) How is the symbolic action of eating bread and drinking wine together a summary of everything that Jesus taught and stood for?

B. Share the group answers with the class. Add new ideas to notebooks.

Session 4 — Keeping the eucharist "alive"

A. After the above lessons, one of my students offered this observation: "That star meant a lot to Mike, but if someone started handing out stars to everyone else, they wouldn't mean anything to people. Isn't that the problem we have getting something out of eucharist?" It is precisely the problem, and one that should be faced.

Write at the board: A symbolic action that is 2000 years old is the center of our Christian religion.

Discuss the following questions:

- What problems follow from that truth written on the board?
- Can the problems be solved?
- What happens to a symbolic action that is repeated over a long period of time?
- How often should we as Christians celebrate the action? (Church law say to observe the eucharistic celebration once a week. Is that often enough? Too often? How often did Mike wear his star? Would once a week, once a month be often enough for him?)
- How can we get back the original meaning of the symbolic action? (Discuss the efforts that have been made to do this since Vatican II.)
- Students often ask "Do I hafta go to Mass?" What's wrong with the question? (There is no answer to it. If Mike had asked his Mom, "Do I have to wear this old star?" how could she have answered him? If the inner love is missing, the external symbolic action is meaningless. But to say the inner love is lacking is to admit to a problem, not to solve one. The problem then becomes: how to create in you the inner love that will make you want to participate in the symbolic action.)

B. Review the definition of a sacrament learned in an earlier unit:
A sacrament is a symbolic action that externalizes an experience of God and that deepens and intensifies the experience.

Apply the definition to eucharist:

- What is the symbolic action? (eating bread and drinking wine together)
- What inner experience of God does it externalize? (the entire experience of Jesus; the experience of belonging to a community of persons who are loved by God the Father, and who love God and one another as Jesus did.)
- How does it deepen the experience? (Christ comes into our hearts to deepen the love he has for us. By sharing in eucharist with others, our love for them is deepened.)

C. Have the students write an essay discussing the statement: A symbolic action that is 2000 years old is the center of our Christian religion.

Session 5 — Why celebrate the eucharist?

A. Discuss: Would you consider yourself a member of a group you never hang around with? Can you consider yourself a Christian if you don't celebrate the eucharist with the community?

As you discuss this question bring out such points as:

This is the thing Jesus asked us to do before he died. Can we fail to do it and still claim to be his friends? Would you consider yourself a member of the band if you were listed as a member but never went to practice? What if you practiced at home every day? What if you went to general practice but never practiced your part on your own? (This discussion should help the class to see that being a Christian is both an individual and a community affair.)

B. Present a chart with the following statements on it. Ask the students to write in their notes whatever solutions they think apply to themselves. They may modify the statements or add to them if they wish.

> I can solve my problems about eucharist by:
> –skipping it altogether
> –going to Mass less frequently
> –going to Mass more frequently
> –really making an effort to get more out of Mass (to put more in)
> –learning more about the eucharist so I understand better what is going on
> –offering to help prepare the celebration of eucharist

C. Share responses and discuss.

Session 6 — The Bread of Life sermon

A. Pass out duplicated copies of the Bread of Life sermon as given on pages 60 and 61. Give the class time to read the script through quietly. Divide the parts among the class so that as many as possible will have a line. Unless you have someone in the class who will do the role of Christ very well, take his role yourself.

B. Act out the script: Have the students "sit around" the room in small groups to simulate a marketplace atmosphere. Jesus will walk in on this scene.

BREAD OF LIFE (John 6: 22–69)[2]

Narrator:	It is the day after the multiplication of the loaves. Most of us were there yesterday. We were part of the crowd that the man Jesus fed with just five loaves of bread and two fish. We wanted to bring Jesus back with us to the city to make him our king, but he didn't want that. He went up into the mountain and hid from the crowd. Later that evening some of us saw his disciples leaving in the boat without him. This morning we've all gathered in the marketplace to see what new developments have happened. Everyone is still talking about the miracle of the bread and fish. Suddenly, Jesus arrives in the marketplace.
First Person:	Here he comes now.
Second Person:	How did he get across the lake? He didn't leave in the boat with his followers.
Third Person:	I took the last boat home. He didn't come with me.
Fourth Person:	(Addressing Jesus) Sir, where did you disappear to yesterday? We were looking all over the mountainside for you.
Jesus:	(Sadly) Yes, you were looking for me. But only because I fed you. Not because you believe in me. You shouldn't be so concerned about perishable things like food. No, spend your energies seeking the eternal life that the Son of Man can give you. For God the Father has sent me for this very purpose.
Fifth person:	What do we have to do to please God?
Jesus:	What God wants is this: That you believe in the one he has sent to you.
Sixth Person:	You must show us more miracles if you want us to believe in you.
First Person:	Sure, just give us free bread every day, like our fathers had while they journeyed in the wilderness.
Second Person:	Yeah, like it says in the holy book, "Moses gave them bread from heaven."
Jesus:	Moses didn't give it to them. My Father did. And now he offers you the true bread from heaven. The true bread is a person—the one sent by God from heaven, and he gives life to the world.
Third Person:	Sir, if that's true, give us this bread every day of our lives.
Jesus:	I am the bread of life. No one coming to me will ever be hungry again. Those believing in me will never thirst.
Narrator:	Then the Jews began murmuring and grumbling to themselves because he claimed to be the Bread from heaven. (Everyone murmurs and grumbles.)

[2]Adapted from *The Living Bible* (Wheaton, Illinois: Tyndale House Publishing, 1971).

(To make copies of this page, use duplicate in tear-out section at back of book.)

Fourth Person: What's he talking about? He is merely Jesus the son of Joseph, we know his father and mother; we know where he is from.

Fifth Person: What is he trying to say? We know he didn't come down from heaven.

Jesus: Don't murmur among yourselves about my saying that. Those the Father speaks to, who learn the truth from him, will understand. Yes, I am the bread of life. There was no real life in that bread from the skies which was given to your fathers in the wilderness, for they all died. But there is such a thing as bread from heaven that will give eternal life to everyone who eats it. And I am that living bread. Anyone who eats this bread will live forever; my flesh is this bread, given to the world.

Narrator: Then the Jews began arguing with each other about what he meant. (Everyone talks—some are getting angry.)

Sixth Person: How can this man give us his flesh to eat?

Jesus: With all the earnestness I possess I tell you this: Unless you eat the flesh of the son of man and drink his blood, you cannot have eternal life within you. My flesh is the true food, and my blood is the true drink. Everyone who eats my flesh and drinks my blood lives in me and I live in him.

First Person: This is very hard to understand.

Second Person: Who can tell what he means?

Third Person: This teaching is too hard.

Fourth Person: Who can listen to this?

Narrator: Jesus knew that his disciples were confused and some were gumbling and complaining.

Jesus: Some of you do not believe. That is what I meant when I said that no one can come to me unless the Father speaks to his heart.

Narrator: At this point many of his disciples turned away and did not follow him anymore.
(Most of the crowd get up and walk away, shaking their heads in disgust. A few stay near Jesus.)

Narrator: Jesus watched them walk away. Then he turned to the Twelve.

Jesus: And you—are you going to leave me also?

Narrator: Peter answered for them all.

Peter: Master, to whom would we go? You alone have the words that give eternal life. And we believe that you are the holy Son of God.

(To make copies of this page, use duplicate in tear-out section at back of book.)

C. After acting the scene, assume the role of a news reporter and interview the crowd. Sample questions are given below:

- Excuse me, sir? Did you just hear the sermon of the prophet from Nazareth?
- What do you think he was trying to say?
- Were you present on the hillside yesterday?
- How do you explain what happened there?
- Have you heard the apostles' report of the things that happened on the lake last night? How do you explain that? They claim he walked across the water, don't they?
- What do you think he meant when he said that those who believe in him will "eat his flesh and drink his blood"?
- Do you still consider yourself one of his followers?
- Do you think he will get his large following back?

Session 7 — New Testament accounts of the institution of the eucharist

A. Explain: The apostles did not understand Christ's words about eating his flesh and drinking his blood. But they stayed with him anyway. Not until the last supper did they see what he meant, and they did not really understand until after the resurrection. Tell the students to open to the Last Supper account in Matthew 26:26–29. Explain that this little paragraph contains many words and phrases that we will not understand unless we hear them with the ears of a Palestinian Jew. Explain what a Hebrew would have understood by:

a) Gave thanks — the great prayer of the chosen people was thanksgiving to God for all the great things he had done for them. The word "eucharist" itself means "Thanksgiving."

b) Broke the bread — breaking bread was a symbol of love and friendship to the Jews. To break bread with someone was to show that you loved him like a member of your own family.

c) Body — this was not a biological term to the Jews, but a personal term. A man *was* his body. When Jesus said "This is my body" it meant: "This is me, my person."

d) Blood — blood to the Jew meant life. It had much the same sense to them that the word "heart" has to us today. (What does "heart" mean in the phrase: I love you with all my heart? It would have made sense for a person in Jesus' time to say, "I love you with all my blood.")

e) New Covenant — the Jews had a covenant with God: he would be their God and protect them and they would be his people and obey his laws. Jesus is making a new Covenant: God will love us as a Father and we will love and serve him as sons and daughters.

f) Sealed with my blood — solemn agreements were sealed in blood, the blood of a lamb was sprinkled on both parties of the agreement as a sign that they were entrusting their lives to one another. Jesus offers his blood to seal the new contract between God and us. (Remind class of the scene in *Tom Sawyer* when Tom and Huck seal an agreement with their blood.)

g) This new Passover — Passover to the Jews meant much the same as our Fourth of July. Had Jesus been talking to us he would have said "This is a new Fourth of July." What would that mean?

    h) Do this in memory of me — the Jews believed that after death a person stayed alive in the underworld as long as someone on earth remembered him. That's why they recited the names of their ancestors as part of their religious feasts. (Cite geneologies in the bible.) What, then did they hear when Jesus said, "Do this to remember me?"

B. Now read the four accounts of the institution. (Mt 26:26–29, Mk 14:22–25, Lk 22:14–20, 1 Cor 11:23–25) Compare them. Point out minor points of difference. How do scholars explain these? Which is most like the one used in Mass today?

Session 8 — Jesus prepares his followers to understand eucharist

A. Explain to the class that Jesus did not spring the idea of eucharist on the disciples at the Last Supper. If we look back through the New Testament we find several events that should have prepared Jesus' followers to understand this great mystery. Look up the following passages and discuss them. Emphasize especially the insights they give us to better understand the eucharist.

    Cana - John 2:1–12
    Miracles of the loaves - Matthew 15:32–39 and 16:5–11
      Mark 6:30–52 and 8:1–10
      Luke 9:10–18
      John 6:1–15
    Walking on water - John 6:16–21
    Bread of Life sermon - John 6:22–71
    Vine and Branches - John 15:1–11

The above readings could also have been assigned as homework. The assignment would then be to read each and to write a sentence or so telling what the passage has to say about eucharist.

B. After the resurrection, the apostles experienced the living presence of Jesus in many ways. This experience was often associated with a meal or the breaking of the bread. Read the two scripture passages below. Some scripture scholars see the two accounts as having to do with the eucharist. See if the class can explain why.

    Emmaus - Luke 24:13–35
    Fishing breakfast - John 21:1–14

C. Assignment: Look up each passage below. After reading all the passages write a short essay on how the church celebrated eucharist in the earliest days.

    Acts 2:42, 2:46, 20:7, 20:11, 27:35
    1 Cor 10:16–17, 11:17–34

Session 9 — Jesus is present in the celebration of the eucharist

A. The mystery of Jesus' presence in the eucharist is one of the most difficult in our faith. It is helpful to analyze the meaning of the word "presence." For this lesson have actual "exhibits" to present one by one and explain. As each is brought forth we ask, "What does presence mean here?"

1. Keys in box. Hold up a small box in which you have secretly placed some keys. Hold it quietly so the keys don't rattle. Then tell the class: My keys are *present* in this box. Do you believe they are there? Why or why not? Put the box down with the mystery unsolved.

2. Parents in a family. Pass around a family picture, and discuss the presence of parents in each child. Say: Someday these parents will no longer be living. Will they still be *present* in the family? When will the family be especially aware of their presence? Explain what presence in the family as a group means as different from presence in each individual.

3. Adoptive parents in children. Pass around a picture of adopted children. Ask: "Are the parents *present* in their adopted children? In what way?"

4. Loved one in letter. I pass around a letter from a sister or brother. What does it mean to say that the writer is *present* in that letter? What do I have to do to experience that presence?

5. Parents in babysitter. One of the students becomes the next exhibit. Say to her: Judy, when you are babysitting, the parents of the little children are *present* in you. What does that mean to you? to the children?

6. Friend in a homemade gift. Sue, you knit a sweater for your boyfriend for Christmas. What does it mean to say you are *present* in the gift? How are you more present than if you had bought the sweater?

7. Teacher in handshake. Dramatize a little situation in which you have a spat with one of the students. When it's all over, you admit that the argument was at least half your fault. The next day when he comes to class, you walk up to him and hold out your hand. What does it mean to say that you are making yourself *present* in that handshake?

B. Ask the students to think over the seven examples of presence and to write down the numbers of those they think say something about how Jesus is present in eucharistic celebration. When they have done this, ask them to circle the one they think best explains Jesus' presence. Call on each to give his or her choice and explain it. Tally their answers. After each of the students has expressed his choice as to the best parallel to the presence of Jesus in eucharist, explain that all of the answers are in some sense *right*, because each exhibit says something about Jesus' presence, but that all of the answers are also *wrong*, because no human example can fully explain the mystery of God's presence to us in eucharist. (The weakest example is number one, the keys in the box, since it refers to a simple spatial kind of presence, although students have found value even in that example. For instance, one student told me that though he couldn't see the keys, he believed they were there because he believed in me.)

C. Now explain that the church teaches that Jesus is really present in eucharist in many ways. (Cf. Constitution on the Sacred Liturgy, #7.) As you present the five ways of his presence, have the students point out which exhibit it corresponds to.

1. Jesus is present in the heart of the individual Christian. (This is something like three above. It is a presence of love and concern.)

2. Jesus is present in the community gathered in his name. (Something like two above.)

3. Jesus is present in his word which is read at Mass. (Something like four above. Point out that one has to read carefully and lovingly to find the person present in a written communique.)

4. Jesus is present in the priest, his official representative. (This is something like five above. Point out that even though you might not be a good babysitter, the

authority of the parents still resides in you. The parents make that presence possible, you don't. Apply to priesthood.)

5. Jesus is present in the consecrated bread and wine—in the eucharistic species. (This is something like six and seven. In both cases the giver puts *himself* into something visible and offers himself to the receiver.)

D. Explain to the class: the presence of Christ in the consecrated bread and wine is a unique and very special kind of presence. The church uses the word Transubstantiation (write the word on the board) to express the mystery of the sacramental presence of Jesus in the eucharistic species. The word means that the bread and wine are changed so that, while the appearances of bread and wine remain, the *reality* (the substance) is the body and blood of Jesus. (See National Catechetical Directory, number 120.)

Session 10

A. Refer again to the seventh exhibit above. Point out that when you offer your hand to the student, there are three things he might do:

1. He could accept your hand and the friendship it offers, and shake hands sincerely.
2. He could turn away and refuse to be reconciled.
3. He could fake it. He could say to himself: "If I'm gonna pass this course, I'd better string the old gal along." He could do the symbolic action, but not really mean it.

Apply this to eucharist. Jesus offers himself to us at each Mass under the appearances of the bread and wine. We can respond in one of three ways. Which way *do* we respond? Discuss.

B. This is also a good time to explain the fallacy in the statement sometimes heard: "If I think Jesus is present in the eucharist, then he is present there for me. If I don't think he's present, then he isn't." Notice that this makes the presence of Jesus depend on my faith, not on his love. To go back to the example: even if the student doesn't believe you are really putting yourself into that handshake, you are there. Your presence depends on you, not on him. Jesus is present in eucharist whether we accept his presence or not, whether we believe or not.

C. Assignment: Refer back to Session 1, the five ways Jesus is present. Tell students to take each of the five and explain a) What can *I* do to better experience his presence in this way? and b) What can *others* do to help me experience him?

Session 11 — The Body of Christ

A. Draw a large circle on the chalk board. Under it write "The Body of Christ." Next to it write these four sentences:

- The Body of Christ was an ordinary human body through which the Son of God was present on earth.
- Jesus reaches the world today through the church; the Christian community is the Body of Christ.
- Every baptized Christian, including me, belongs to the Body of Christ.
- The Eucharistic bread consecrated at Mass is the Body of Christ.

Ask the class to study the four statements to see whether they really can say "Yes, I believe that!" about each of them. When they have had a few minutes to think quietly, tell them that if they really believe the statements, they should walk up and write their names in the circle. (Don't say any more. Quietly wait to see what will happen.)

B. When it looks like all have signed who are going to, discuss the experience? Could they sign for some of the statements and not others? Do they believe some more strongly than others? How did they feel about being called on to do this publicly? Have they ever done such a thing before, made a public commitment of their faith in those basic truths?

Take off on the last question to explain that that is precisely what they do, or ought to do, each time they walk up to receive Holy Communion. They publicly proclaim, in both word and action, their belief in, and acceptance of, the Body of Christ. When the priest holds up the host and says to you "The Body of Christ," he is really saying:

> Do you believe this is the Body of Christ?
> Do you want it to be the Body of Christ?
> Do you accept the rest of these people here as the Body of Christ?
> Do you want to belong to the Body of Christ?
> Are you willing to live like the Body of Christ?
> Will you do the work of the Body of Christ?
> Would you be willing to die like the Body of Christ?

And to all this we answer "Amen," which is a very emphatic way of saying yes. And to seal our commitment we eat the bread which is the Body of Christ. No wonder Paul says, "If anyone does not recognize the meaning of the Lord's body when he eats the bread and drinks from the cup, he brings judgment on himself when he eats and drinks" (1 Cor 11:29).

C. Give the class time to write some feedback statements and share them:

> The thing that struck me about today's class was...
> I am confused about...
> I am not sure if I believe...
> I have really decided to...

D. Assignment: Imagine Christ asking you the questions listed above. Write him your answer. Explain to him the problems you have doing all of those things.

Session 12 — Do I have to go to Mass on Sunday?

A. Write the question on the board and ask each student to write his answer to it? Share their answers.

B. Recall a previous lesson on the various levels of morality. (See Unit 2. If you haven't taught that lesson, now is a good time to do it.) List the six levels on the board. How would the question "Do I have to go to Mass?" be answered for a person operating on each level?

1. Spanking level	Yes, I have to go to Mass or my parents won't let me out of the house all day.
2. Lollipop level	If I want to go to Heaven someday, I have to go to Mass now.

3. Good-boy (girl) level	What would my parents think if I didn't go? It wouldn't look good.
4. Law-and-order level	If I'm going to play on God's team I have to play by God's rules. He only asks an hour.
5. Conviction level	I don't feel like going, but I certainly owe God this little bit for all he does for me.
6. Love level	God is so good to me! What is one hour of worship in response to so much love.

C. Point out that the first two levels are really answered by someone else for me. The decision is made by someone else and either forced on me, or used to bribe me. The teen who says "I don't get anything out of it" is operating on that level. He is expecting some reward, even if it's just the reward of a good feeling for having gone. Making the Mass "cool" with a lot of gimmicks can also be a form of lollipop.

The next two levels also have the decision coming from the outside but more subtly. The youth who skips Mass because his buddies do, who doesn't participate because he doesn't want to look too holy, who looks to see who else is going to communion before he gets up to go, is also operating on the good-boy level. He is simply seeking the approval of someone other than his parents.

In the last two levels, the decision is internal. I decide to worship at Mass because I see a value in it. (This is not the same as feeling good about it. I do what I see as right no matter how I feel about it.) The difference between five and six is joy. In five I decide out of a sense of duty. I'll do it if it kills me. In six, I decide out of love. Love always finds its gift too small. Love says, "What more can I do?"

D. If you have taught the lesson on Parent-Child-Adult (Unit 2) point out that one and two appeal to the child, three and four to the parent, and five and six to the adult.

E. When someone asks me the question above, I like to answer, "I don't think you should be permitted to go to Mass." Then I explain that the early church was very fussy about who they let in to celebrate the eucharist. Only committed practicing Christians were allowed. Those who were learning about the faith but hadn't dedicated their lives to it yet, were asked to leave after the Creed. Ask the students if they think the church should revive that practice. Under those standards, would they be permitted to stay for the solemn part of the Mass? Supposing next Sunday the pastor announced after the Creed: "The rest of the Mass is a sacred rite reserved for dedicated Christians. Anyone who is not serious about living up to his Christian commitment is asked to leave now." What do you think would happen? What would you do? Your friends? Your parents? Would you advise your pastor to do that? Why or why not?

F. Explain: Our aim as parents and teachers is to have our children and students make a conviction level (or a love level) decision about Sunday Mass. What is the right way and the wrong way to bring this about? When this has been discussed for a few minutes, point out that parents can fail on either extreme.

Too little pressure ◄————————————————► Too much pressure

Have the students explain what will happen in either extreme above. See if they can describe for you the happy medium.

G. To help the students see where they are in answering that question, break the question down into the questions listed below. Have students write their own conviction level answers to each question.

Why worship God at all?

Why belong to an organized church with organized forms of worship?

Why belong to the church whose central form of worship is the Mass?

Why celebrate Mass once a week?

Why on Sunday?

You could give the students answers to the questions, but you (and they) will be surprised at the quality of their own answers. Work together for a class answer to each of the questions. Notice that each answer is based on a resolution of the problem before it.

H. Refer back to the answer written to the question in A. Ask the students to write a short essay answering the question again. They should incorporate in their essay any new insights they learned in this session.

Session 13 — A Prayer Sharing on eucharist based on *The Little Prince*

A. Have the class meet in an informal chapel or some other cozy setting where they can sit around you on the floor. Duplicate copies of the excerpt from Saint-Exupery's *The Little Prince*.[1] (See pages 69–70.)

Tell the class a bit about the story. (You will have to read the book, if you haven't done so already.) Then read the excerpt to them. After you have read it, pass out the duplicated copies. Tell the students to read it again quietly, circling any lines or phrases that they think have something to say about eucharist. Give them plenty of time to do this.

Call on individuals to tell the group what they circled and why. (I have always been amazed at the depth of sharing this little story provokes.)

B. Pass out another paper on which you have written something like this:

Jesus—like the fox—is asking you to be his friend. But as the fox said, friendship takes a lot of time and a lot of patience. "Come every day," Jesus says, "and sit quietly with me. If you do, you will come a little closer each day."

I would like you to seriously consider spending some special time with Jesus every day, or at least several times a week. Just come and be with him. A very good time would be at daily Mass. Or you could find some time each day to spend alone in chapel or in church letting Jesus "tame" you.

Write down all the reasons you can think of why you could *not* make a decision to do that.

Now write down all the reasons you can think of why you *could* and *should*.

Now study both sets of reasons, and decide! Write your decision in the form of a prayer. You will not be sharing these prayers with us. They are just between you and Jesus.

C. Close with a quiet praying time in which we all pray for one another that we will really do the thing we promised Christ on those papers. Tell the students to put the papers away in a safe spot, and someday to get them out again to check up on their progress. Or you could have them sealed or stapled shut. You collect them and promise to return them in a month or so.

[1]Abridged from *The Little Prince* by Antoine De Saint-Exupery. Copyright 1943, 1971 by Harcourt Bruce Jovanovich, Inc. Reprinted by permission of the publisher.

The Little Prince (excerpts)

It was then that the fox appeared.

"Good morning," said the fox.

"Good morning," the little prince responded politely, although when he turned around he saw nothing.

"I am right here," the voice said, "under the apple tree."

"Who are you?" asked the little prince, and added, "You are very pretty to look at."

"I am a fox," the fox said.

"Come and play with me," proposed the little prince. "I am so unhappy."

"I cannot play with you," the fox said. "I am not tamed."

"Ah! Please excuse me," said the little prince.

But, after some thought, he added:

"What does that mean—'tame'?"

. . . .

"It is an act too often neglected," said the fox. "It means to establish ties."

"'To establish ties'?"

"Just that," said the fox. "To me, you are still nothing more than a little boy who is just like a hundred thousand other little boys. And I have no need of you. And you, on your part, have no need of me. To you, I am nothing more than a fox like a hundred thousand other foxes. But if you tame me, then we shall need each other. To me, you will be unique in all the world. To you, I shall be unique in all the world . . ."

"I am beginning to understand," said the little prince. "There is a flower . . . I think that she has tamed me . . ."

"It is possible," said the fox. "On the earth one sees all sorts of things."

. . . .

But he came back to his idea.

"My life is very monotonous," he said. "I hunt chickens; men hunt me. All the chickens are just alike, and all the men are just alike. And, in consequence, I am a little bored. But if you tame me, it will be as if the sun came to shine on my life. I shall know the sound of a step that will be different from all the others. Other steps send me hurrying back underneath the ground. Yours will call me, like music, out of my burrow. And then look: you see the grain-fields down yonder? I do not eat bread. Wheat is of no use to me. The wheat fields have nothing to say to me. And that is sad. But you have hair that is the color of gold. Think how wonderful that will be when you have tamed me! The grain, which is also golden, will bring me back the thought of you. And I shall love to listen to the wind in the wheat . . ."

The fox gazed at the little prince, for a long time.

"Please, tame me!" he said.

"I want to very much," the little prince replied. "But I have not much time. I have friends to discover and a great many things to understand."

"One only understands the things that one tames," said the fox. "Men have no more time to understand anything. They buy things all ready made at the shops. But there is no shop anywhere where one can buy friendship, and so men have no friends any more. If you want a friend, tame me . . ."

"What must I do, to tame you?" asked the little prince.

"You must be very patient," replied the fox. "First you will sit down at a little distance from me—like that—in the grass. I shall look at you out of the corner of my eye, and you will say nothing. Words are the source of misunderstandings. But you will sit a little closer to me, every day..."

. . . .

So the little prince tamed the fox. And when the hour of his departure drew near—

"Ah," said the fox, "I shall cry."

"It is your own fault," said the little prince. "I never wished you any sort of harm, but you wanted me to tame you..."

"Yes, that is so," said the fox.

"But now you are going to cry!" said the little prince.

"Yes, that is so," said the fox.

"Then it has done no good at all!"

"It has done me good," said the fox, "because of the color of the wheat fields." And then he added:

"Go and look again at the roses. You will understand now that yours is unique in all the world. Then come back to say goodbye to me, and I will make you a present of a secret."

The little prince went away to look again at the roses.

"You are not at all like my rose," he said. "As yet you are nothing. No one has tamed you, and you have tamed no one. You are like my fox when I first knew him. He was only a fox like a hundred thousand other foxes. But I have made him my friend, and now he is unique in all the world."

And the roses were very much embarrassed.

"You are beautiful, but you are empty," he went on. "One could not die for you. To be sure an ordinary passerby would think that my rose looked just like you—the rose that belongs to me. But in herself alone she is more important than all the hundreds of other roses: because it is she that I have watered; because it is she that I have put under the glass globe; because it is she that I have sheltered behind the screen; because it is for her that I have killed the caterpillars (except the two or three that we saved to become butterflies); because it is she that I have listened to, when she grumbled, or boasted, or even sometimes when she said nothing. Because she is *my* rose."

And he went back to meet the fox.

"Goodbye," he said.

"Goodbye," said the fox. "And now here is my secret, a very simple secret: It is only with the heart that one can see rightly; what is essential is invisible to the eye."

"What is essential is invisible to the eye," the little prince repeated, so that he would be sure to remember.

. . . .

Session 14 — Celebrating Eucharist

A. Plan a celebration of the eucharist to close the unit. This should preferably be a small group celebration in a comfortable informal setting. Although it would also be valuable for the class to plan a Sunday Mass for the entire parish.

B. The students can make contributions to the Mass in the following ways:

- Prepare the setting: altar, banners, candles, decorations.
- Select the music, practice it, and perform it.
- Pick the readings. It is good to have one religious nonscriptural reading besides the two required scripture readings.
- (The *Little Prince* reading above could be used, for instance.)
- Prepare a slide show to accompany the readings or as a communion meditation.
- Prepare a creed (See Unit 1). Read it at the Mass.
- Prepare the litany-type prayers for the prayers of forgiveness, the prayers of petition, and the thanksgiving after communion. Samples of each are given below:

   Prayers for forgiveness:
   > For all the times we have celebrated the eucharist grudgingly or half-heartedly, we ask your forgiveness, Lord.
   > Response: *Lord, have mercy.*

   Offertory petition:
   > For the people in the world who have never heard of Christ and his church, we pray to the Lord.
   > Response: *Lord, hear our prayer.*

   Prayers of thanksgiving:
   > I would like to thank God for my parents who have brought me up to know him and to love him.
   > Response: *We thank you, Lord.*

   (It is good to have five or six items in each of the above litanies.)

C. If there is not a long time to prepare for the Mass, a degree of participation can be achieved by having the creed and the three litanies above prepared just before Mass. Give out sheets with the format for each litany to individuals or small groups and ask them to be prepared to share one of the prayers at the appropriate part of the Mass. Format for the creed would be:

   I believe in God, who ... or   I believe that God....

If your group is small enough, and comfortable with one another, the prayers at these parts of the Mass could be contributed spontaneously.

Unit 6

Sin and the Sacrament of Reconciliation

The purpose of this unit is to help adolescents face the reality of sin in their own lives and understand that the sacrament of reconciliation can play an important role in their growth as persons and as Christians.[1]

The unit first builds a description of a "good person" based on the moral principles outlined in the 10 Commandments. It then helps the teens to see that each individual is, to a large degree, responsible for the kind of person he or she becomes. The young people are encouraged to examine their daily decisions to see whether these are building the kind of persons they want to be. The teens are helped to discover the patterns of sinfulness in both their personal and their social lives.

Next they are guided to see that they can and should do something about personal and communal sin. The sacrament of reconciliation is presented as a powerful symbolic action through which God offers us, as individuals and as a group, forgiveness for our sins and the strength and courage needed to do something about them.

Session 1 — Where do you stand on penance now?

A. Write on the board one at a time the unfinished sentences listed below. Give the class time to finish the sentence, then call on several students to share their answers. Be sure to honor their right to pass. When one sentence has been thoroughly discussed, write the next on the board. If you do not have time for all of the sentences, be sure to do the last one. Do not at this time attempt to answer the problems these questions will raise. This is simply an opportunity for you and the class to see clearly what the problems concerning this sacrament are, and they are many. You may tell the students that it is your hope that the unit you are about to begin will answer their questions.

Unfinished sentences:

- What I don't understand about confession is. . . .
- My best experience of the sacrament of penance was. . . .
- I think this sacrament could be improved by. . . .
- What I find hardest about confession is. . . .
- The last time I went to confession was. . . .
- I am (very, somewhat, slightly, not at all) open to the possibility that this unit might help me to re-evaluate the role of confession in my life, because. . . .

B. Ask the students to write their own definition of sin, and to list five things that they know teens their age do that they consider sinful. Share these responses.

[1]See author's articles "Teenagers and Confession" in *Catechist* 8, February, 1975, pp. 30–35, and "Teens and the Ten Commandments" in *Catechist* 11, September, 1978, p. 40.

Session 2 — Goodness

A. Explain to the students that we cannot understand penance unless we understand sin, and we cannot understand sin unless we understand goodness. Divide the class into groups of four. Give each group a large sheet of paper and a magic marker. Have them write at the top of the sheet "A good person is one who..." and list on the paper as many things as they can that would complete the sentence. Hang these papers up for future reference.

B. The material that follows is quite complex but extremely important.

1) Explain: A good person is one who has a proper relationship with
   –himself or herself
   –others
   –God

2) Draw a circle on the board to represent self. Explain: There are five elements that each human person needs in order to be a whole human being. Each of us has a right to these elements. We can insist upon our right to them, can demand that the people around us respect them. These are: (Write each of the five things in the circle. Explain each as you write it.)

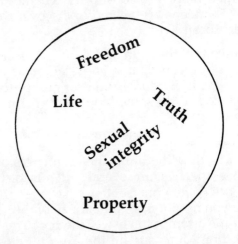

Freedom: This is one of our greatest gifts. God has given each of us a free will, the power to choose, to make our own decisions, to determine for ourselves what we want to do with our lives.

Truth: The second great gift to the human person is our intellect, the power to understand, to know the truth about ourself and our world.

Life: This gift includes life itself, physical and mental health, and all the things we need to live, e.g., air, water, food, sunshine.

Sexual integrity: This includes the right to determine one's own state in life: marriage, single life, or religious consecration. It includes the right to raise a family, to sexual privacy, etc.

Property: Everyone has a right to a certain amount of property—to have some things that we can call our own, a house to live in, land, and space.

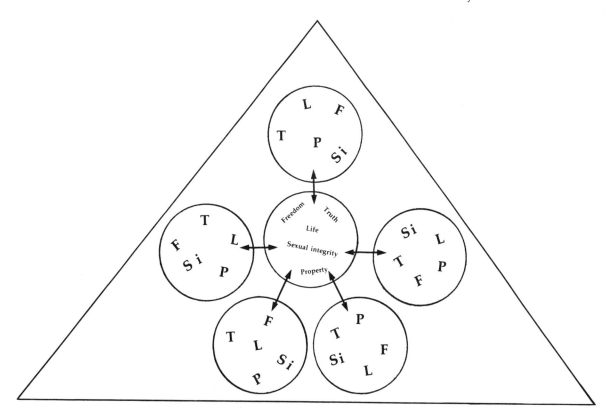

3) Explain: But I am not the only person in my world. I live in a community of persons (draw circles surrounding the center circle) each of whom has the same rights to the five basic elements as I do. Say to one student: This circle represents you, Joe. What are your five basic rights? (Write the initials of the five in each circle, asking a different student to say them for you each time.)

4) Connect the circles with double arrows explaining again that each of us owes these rights to others and can demand them from others. A good person is one who respects his own freedom, truth, life, property, and sexual integrity and who respects and defends these rights in everyone else.

5) A good person also has a proper relationship with God. He realizes that there is within himself, within all other persons, within all of creation a power that is greater than all of creation. (Draw a large triangle that includes all of the circles.) The simplest most basic response to that person, God, is:

   1. Acknowledge that he exists. Admit that my own life and my world came from someone far greater than I.
   2. Respect him. Respect the things and persons, the buildings and books that are dedicated to him. Respect his name.
   3. Worship him. Thank him for the things he gives me. Gather with others to thank and worship him together. Praise him—tell him how great his world is and how much I appreciate it.

6) Summarize numbers 1–5 by writing on the board:

   A good person is one who:

   Respects freedom and authority.

Respects truth.
Respects life.
Respects sexuality.
Respects property.
Acknowledges that God exists.
Respects him.
Worships and thanks him.

7) Have the students look at the list. Tell them they have seen it before. When they recognize the list they should raise their hands, but not say anything. If the hands are slow in going up, give a few more hints: the list is 4000 years old, you could find it in the bible, and once it was written on tablets of stone. When everyone knows that they are looking at the 10 Commandments, have someone go to the board and number the things listed to correspond to the commandments. Notice that there will be two numbers, six and nine, for sexuality, and two, seven and 10, for property.

8) Assignment: Write the 10 Commandments as they appeared in the old catechism (get your parents to help you). Next to each, write the short form used above. Study both forms.

Session 3

A. Review the entire lesson above. Ask someone to put the diagram from yesterday's lesson on the board and to explain it with the class's help. Call on individuals to recite the 10 Commandments, long and short form. (Make this a game not a chore.)

B. Discuss the difference between respect and love. (Love goes beyond but always includes respect.) Then explain that Jesus elevated the commandments from the level of respect to the level of love. "Thou shalt love the Lord thy God . . ." tells us that the basic law of Christianity is that a person should love God
love others
love himself.

Show how this corresponds to the outline above: good persons respect themselves, others, and God.

C. Write on the homework paper above the commandment of Jesus: You shall love the Lord your God with your whole heart, with your whole soul, with your whole mind, and with your whole strength. And you shall love your neighbor as yourself.

Assign for memorization:
The long form of the 10 Commandments
The short form (Session 2, number 6)
The commandment of Jesus

Tell class that they will be expected to write these from memory next class and in a future test.

Session 4

A. Duplicate and distribute charts like the one on page 77. These will be used to review and expand on the material presented in Sessions 2 and 3.

Diagram

To be a whole human being, every person needs:	SELF — Persons who respect this quality in themselves would:	OTHERS — Persons who respect this quality in others would:

GOD   The most basic relationship with God requires one to:

Jesus elevated the whole moral code to three simple rules:

LOVE OTHERS

LOVE SELF

LOVE GOD

(To make copies of this page, use duplicate in tear-out section at back of book.)

B. Review the diagram from Session 2 and its meaning—have students draw it in the upper left hand corner of the chart.

C. Work together at filling in the remaining boxes. The question is: what does a person *do* who respects God, self, and others. The kinds of things that could be listed in the boxes are given below:

RESPECT FOR GOD

A person who acknowledges that God exists will:
  –make God the most important person in his or her life
  –trust that the world is in good hands
  –be willing to love all persons as brothers and sisters
  –value everything as a gift from God
  –realize that he or she owes life itself to someone (God).
A person who respects God will:
  –use his name respectfully
  –respect persons, buildings, books that are dedicated to him.
A person who worships God properly will:
  –pray privately each day
  –gather with others to worship on Sunday
  –praise him always for his beautiful world.

Respect for Self

A person who respects and values his own freedom will:
  –make his own decisions, not be led by the crowd
  –stand up for what he believes
  –avoid drugs and intoxicants that would deprive him of his ability to make free choices
  –seek advice in making decisions
  –fight to defend his freedom if necessary.
A person who respects and values his own truth will:
  –learn all he can about his world, himself, God
  –be open to new ideas
  –value his education, get the most out of school
  –admit his own mistakes, be honest with himself
  –avoid drugs or intoxicants that would keep him from thinking clearly.
A person who respects and values his own life will:
  –get enough sleep and exercise
  –eat sensibly, avoiding over-eating and over-dieting
  –drive carefully, avoid unnecessary dangers
  –avoid overindulgence in such things as alcohol, cigarettes.
A person who respects and values his own sexuality will:
  –have a correct understanding of the sexual mechanisms of his body
  –learn to control his own sexual drives, to use them truly, lovingly
  –use his sexuality properly
  –avoid books and movies that treat sexuality lightly or irreverently.

A person who respects and values his own property will:
  –avoid waste and superfluity
  –take care of his things, keep them clean and in order
  –work hard to earn the things he wants and needs
  –budget wisely and save money.

Respect for Others

  A person who respects and values the freedom of others will:
    –respect authority, the power that balances one man's freedom against another's. (It may take further clarification to see the relationship between freedom and authority. Ask the class to consider what would happen if everyone always did just what he wanted to do. Help them to see that society has set up laws as a way of regulating freedom—everyone has to give up a little of his freedom to preserve the freedom of others.)
    –respect a person's right to be different
    –obey the laws of family, city, country
    –respect authority persons: parents, teachers and policemen.
  A person who respects and values another's right to truth will:
    –tell the truth at all times
    –avoid disrupting classes, and such things that would keep others from learning
    –avoid cheating and other kinds of dishonesty
    –pay school taxes
    –give his or her own children a good education.
  A person who respects the life of others will:
    –drive carefully
    –be careful of air, water, land, and other resources
    –respect all forms and ages of human life
    –protect nature and wildlife, follow hunting and conservation rules.
  A person who respects the sexuality of others will:
    –avoid "using" relationships (see Unit 9)
    –dress modestly, so as not to be a cause of temptation to others
    –respect the contract of marriage
    –avoid teasing and flirting that would arouse the sexual drive of another.
  A person who respects the property of others will:
    –not steal or damage property
    –avoid mistreating public property
    –pay his share for the things owned by all (taxes).

Session 5 — Blueprint for my life

A. Give out duplicates of the form on page 81. Explain: A person who wants to build a house begins by making a blueprint—a design of all the features to build into the home. Then he begins, step by step, to do all the things he must do to put those features into his building.

We all have a "blueprint" in our minds and hearts of the kind of person we want to be. But the bricks of life we lay by the things we do every day don't always agree with that ideal self. This form helps us to examine our blueprint and how well we are following it. Mark the form using the following code:

+ building going well
− building going poorly
0 not in my plans at all

Double pluses (++) and double minuses (− −) could be used to indicate areas of special strength or weakness. Tell the students that this exercise will not be shared.

B. When they have filled out the sheet, have them list three things they learned about themselves by doing that exercise. Use these statements as a basis for discussion.

C. Have them study the paper once more. Then write: As a result of this study I have resolved that... Tell them that these answers will not be shared.

BLUEPRINT FOR MY LIFE — I WANT TO BE ONE WHO....

Personal Integrity
(the person in himself)

FREEDOM
I want to be a person who
___ is really free
___ makes his own decisions
___ has his own set of values
___ stands up for what he believes
___ is independent
___ has strong will-power

TRUTH
I want to be a person who
___ knows the truth about himself
___ knows the truth about his world
___ understands his God and religion
___ is able to reason out problems
___ has a good education
___ can accept failure
___ is honest with himself
___ is open to new ideas
___ admits his own mistakes
___ says what he means

LIFE AND SEXUALITY
I want to be a person who
___ is mentally and physically whole
___ has a healthy body
___ has a healthy mind
___ doesn't overdo it
___ is good looking
___ understands his own sexuality
___ respects his own body
___ has control of his sexual self

PROPERTY
I want to be a person who
___ has things he can call his own
___ is financially set
___ has a good career or job
___ has the kind of house, car, clothes he wants

LOVE OF SELF
I want to be a person who
___ has many true friends
___ gets along well with others

___ is well-adjusted
___ has a good sense of humor
___ is able to influence others
___ is loved
___ is treated with respect
___ is easy-going and carefree
___ has a don't quit attitude
___ gives his best at everything
___ is successful
___ is somebody
___ is real, not fake
___ has no enemies

Justice and Love
(the person in relationship)

GOD: ACKNOWLEDGE, RESPECT, WORSHIP
I want to be a person who
___ acknowledges God as his Lord
___ really prays
___ is grateful to God for everything
___ worships God freely and lovingly
___ wants to know God better
___ is close to God
___ gives a gift of himself to God
___ lives the Christian life fully
___ respects God's name, buildings
___ accepts God's help in his life

OTHERS: RESPECT FOR FREEDOM AND AUTHORITY
I want to be a person who
___ respects the freedom of every person
___ respects and loves his parents
___ respects church authorities
___ respects teachers, policemen, and others in authority.
___ obeys the laws of city and country,
___ is just
___ works with others

RESPECT FOR LIFE AND SEXUALITY
I want to be a person who
___ respects all human life
___ protects nature and wildlife,
___ drives safely
___ is careful of water, air, and land
___ respects the sexuality of others
___ respects the contract of marriage

RESPECT FOR PROPERTY
I want to be a person who
___ respects the property of others
___ takes care of public property
___ does not steal or damage property
___ pays his share (taxes, dues)

RESPECT FOR TRUTH
I want to be a person who
___ can be trusted
___ tells the truth
___ is honest in his dealings with others

LOVE OF OTHERS
I want to be a person who
___ gives of himself for others
___ respects the feelings of others
___ is kind and considerate
___ is unselfish
___ is grateful
___ cares for the sick, lonely, deprived
___ brings joy to others
___ believes in others
___ listens
___ cares
___ knows how to really love

+ building going well
- building going poorly
0 not in my plans at all

Session 6 — Sin

A. Make a list on the board of all the things the class can think of that are sinful. List whatever is suggested, whether all agree that it is a sin or not.

B. Explain: Everyone wants to be good, but everyone sins. Why is this?

   - I want to be free, make my own decisions; yet I let some puny kid talk me into doing something I shouldn't do and would rather not do.
   - I want to respect sex; yet I tell, and laugh at, dirty jokes.
   - I want to love my parents; yet I get angry and stalk out of the room when asked to do a little thing like help with dishes.
   - I want to have a healthy body; yet I am really getting hooked on cigarettes.
   - I want to be whole, strong, true, loving; I am selfish, mean, lazy, dishonest. WHY?

C. Present the following six reasons for why we do the sinful things we do. Put the italicized words on the board as you explain each point.

   1) I make a *mistake*. I choose to do something I sincerely think is good. I find out later that it was really bad, that it hurt me or someone else to have done it.
   2) I choose a *lesser good over a greater good*. For example, it will be good for me to get an A on that test; it will also be good to be honest and not copy from the "brain" sitting beside me. Given the choice between two good things, a good mark and being honest, I choose the lesser good, the good mark.
   3) I choose something that is *good for me but bad for you*. It will be really good for me to have that $10 bill lying on your desk. Too bad for you that the money happens to be yours.
   4) I choose to do something that is *good now* that *might be bad later*. Drinking, smoking, speeding, playing with sex all fit into this category. When I decide to get involved with these things I am only thinking about the immediate good feeling that I want to get from them. I try to shut out of my mind that *possible evil* that I have been warned about.
   5) I choose to do something that is *good now* that will *definitely* be *bad later*. Drunkenness, premarital sex, hard drugs fit into this category. I know when I do the act that evil will follow.
   6) I choose to do something bad *just because it is bad*. Revenge, vandalism, black magic, would fit here.

D. Refer back to the list made in B. Have students give each sin listed a number to indicate which category it would fit under. (Many will fit into more than one category.)

E. Discuss the degree of sinfulness to each of the six points above. Lead the class to see that:

   1) A mistake is never a sin. When I decided to do the act I thought it was good. However, we must be careful of rationalizing, trying to convince ourselves that we think a thing is good when in our heart we know it is not.
   2) Choosing a lesser good over a greater good may be a sin or not, depending on the two good things involved. The one listed above is a sin. If I choose between the good of watching TV and the good of doing my homework, it might not be.

3) Choosing to do what is good for me but bad for someone else is almost always sinful, because I am hurting someone else.

4 & 5) Four and five should be looked at together. The students will see that doing something that is good now but will have definite evil consequences is definitely sinful. They will have trouble deciding whether four is a sin or not. It helps to see that four and five are two ends of a continuum—one cigarette is not sinful, three packs a day probably is; one beer is not sinful, getting drunk every night is; a little flirting is not sinful, "going all the way" is. Many of the choices the teens must make today fit someplace on that continuum between four and five. It will often be difficult for the individual to decide just where. If he is sincere about wanting to be good, he will not let himself get anywhere near the five end of the line, and may want to stay off it altogether.

6) Choosing to do evil just because it is evil is always sinful.

F. With the understanding they now have, ask the students to define sin. They should come up with something like this: Sin is a decision I make freely to do something I know is wrong. Sin weakens or destroys some kind of goodness in me, in another person, or in a relationship between myself and others or between myself and God.

Session 7 — What can I do about the sin in my life?

A. Give the students half sheets of paper. Tell them that what they are about to write should be printed or written in a manner other than their usual handwriting so that the papers will remain completely anonymous. Tell them the papers will be collected and read aloud.

Have the students write on the paper: The sin in my life is . . . and list two or three areas of sinfulness in their lives. They should list things that a) they themselves do b) deliberately and c) repeatedly d) that they know are wrong, e) that are in some way going against the basic rules of respect for God, for others, or for self.

While the students are writing, you should do likewise.

B. Collect the papers and shuffle them well. The students should be aware that your paper is included in the pack. Then read the papers aloud to the class. (If the group is not large enough to assure anonymity, you may choose not to read them aloud.)

Ask several students to respond to the reading: How did it feel to hear their sins read out loud? How did they feel when they heard all of those sins? How do they think God reacts to all that sinfulness?

C. Ask one student:

What can you do about the sin in your life? Can you change? Supposing you were the one who wrote that your sin is the rotten way you treat your dad? What can you do about that? Supposing your sin is getting drunk every weekend? Can you change that? How does a person go about getting rid of a pattern of sinfulness?

D. You take a good look at your life and you see sin there. What can you do about it? One at a time, list on the blackboard the possibilities given below. As you write each, discuss how effective it would be to help someone get rid of an area of sinfulness that he or she wants out of his or her life. (Write only italicized words on the board.)

1 - You could do *nothing*. (Emphasize: not only will the sin not go away, but it will probably get worse.)

2 - You could resolve to do something about that sin—*tomorrow*. (The students will be quick to point out that tomorrow never comes.)

3 - You could *seriously resolve* to do something to change that sin now, or the very next time the temptation comes along. (Call on several students to see if that would work for them.)

4 - You could *talk to God* about the problem. You could ask him to help you to really keep your resolution to change. (The students will not find this much more helpful than the last mentioned. They will say things like "How do you know if God is even listening?")

5 - You could *talk to someone* who would understand your problem, who would give you guidance on how to overcome the habit of sin you are concerned about. (Ask how many have a "someone" in their world with whom they can share really deep and personal problems of this kind.)

6 - You could combine three, four and five in the sacrament of reconciliation.

E. Ask several students: Supposing you did six. Supposing you took the sins you have written on this paper, resolved to do something about them, prayed, and then brought your sins to the priest for guidance, prayer, and forgiveness. Would that make a difference in what you actually <u>did</u> about that area of sinfulness?

F. Recall with the class the first day of this unit. In answer to the question "What I don't get about confession . . .," at least half of the class probably wrote, "I don't understand why we have to go through a priest. Why can't we go straight to God?" The answer to that question is in Step E. Your students have probably agreed that talking to God about their sin is not going to help them to really change. They are going to need a more tangible help than that. And that is precisely why Christ gave us this sacrament—we often need to externalize our sorrow and our desire to improve in a symbolic action before we can get the power and courage and resolve we need to really change. (I have found that this lesson nearly always has a powerful effect on the students. For some of them it is the first time in their lives that they have understood what the sacrament of penance is all about.)

Session 8 — More on forgiveness of sin

A. What does it mean to have sin forgiven? Some people still think of sin as the black X you get on your soul when you break one of God's laws. You tell God you're sorry and he erases the X. But if sin is seen as something much more real than that—as a pattern of destructive decisions that a person is making, then getting rid of sin is a lot more complex than just getting a bad spot erased. The sin isn't gone until the pattern of sinfulness is changed.

B. Let's look at the steps needed to get rid of an area of sinfulness:

1) I have to see if there is an area of sin in my life. It is easy to go on day after day without ever taking time out to examine my life to see if some of my decisions are contrary to the kind of person God and I want me to be.

2) I have to admit that what I am doing is sinful, that it is damaging myself, or another person, or a relationship. And I have to admit that this is my own fault, or at least partly my fault.

3) I have to really want to change. Very often the sin is a source of fun or pleasure that I don't really want to give up.

4) I have to do something about it. I have to return the stolen money, or repair the broken relationship, or stop going out with that person, or quit going to those Saturday night booze parties. This will take a great deal of courage and determination.

There are biblical names for each of the obstacles listed here

1) Failure to even *see* my own sinfulness: BLINDNESS

2) Refusal to *admit* that it is my fault: PRIDE

3) Knowing that I am sinning but not caring, not wanting to change: HARDNESS OF HEART

4) Inability to do anything about my sins: WEAKNESS, FEAR.

Jesus came to take away our sins. That means he has to help us with those four things. Which is the biggest problem, the biggest obstacle? Discuss.

C. If I want to get rid of the sin in my life, I must first know there is sin there, then admit to it, want to change, and finally really change. I can do these four things alone, or in prayer with God, or with the help of a friend, or in the sacrament of reconciliation. Let's look at some of the advantages for doing them through the sacrament:

1) If I examine my life before God, I will be much more honest about it. I can fool myself but I can't fool him. Also the fact that I have decided to go to confession forces me to take time to look for sin in my life, which I might not have done otherwise. (Ask students when was the last time, before this unit, they took time to look for a pattern of sin in their lives.)

2) It is much more effective to admit my sin out loud than just to admit it to myself. (Discuss reasons for this.)

3) I don't always know how to go about changing a pattern of sin. The priest will give me the help I need, and encourage me to really try.

4) I do not have in myself the power to heal a sinful life. God can and will give me this power. He will give me the courage that comes from knowing I am loved, and the peace of knowing I am doing right. In the sacrament he offers me this forgiveness, love, and courage in a tangible, visible form.

D. Refer again to the "pack" of sins from the last session. Ask each student to think about one of the sins he or she wrote on the paper.

- Say to one of the students: You're thinking about one of the areas of sinfulness in your life. In order to get rid of that sin you would first have to *see* that it is sinful, *admit* that you are doing it, *want to change*, and then have the courage to *do something* about changing. Which of those four things would you say is keeping you from getting rid of that sin? Is there something you *can* do about that? *Will* do about it? Can you promise yourself that you *will* take steps to change that area of sinfulness? Starting when? Will the sacrament of reconciliation help?

- Carry on similar dialogues with various other students. This dialogue understandably takes a good deal of skill, sensitivity, and respect on the part of the teacher, and an atmosphere of openness and respect to which the whole class must contribute. At no time does the student reveal what sin he or she is thinking about.

Session 9 — Ways of celebrating penance

A. The sacrament of penance can be celebrated in various ways

    1) Communal penance: emphasis here is on sins committed by the community, sins we all have a share in. For teenagers this would be things like drinking parties, cutting others down, lack of seriousness in study. It would be much easier to change these things if the whole gang would resolve together to change them. A communal penance service is a good chance to think seriously about sin, to admit to yourself and God that you have sinned, and to make a private resolve to change. Since there is not usually much time, it is not a good time to get help from the priest in changing a pattern of sinfulness.

    2) Private confession face-to-face: If any students have had this experience, have them tell the class about it. If not, you yourself should try to convince the students of the added value of the person-to-person contact. It takes a bit of getting used to, but once you've tried it, you won't go back to the old way.

    3) Private confession behind a screen: If a student feels more comfortable with this form, fine. Encourage the students to make this a personal experience not a rattling off of a grocery list of sins. The priest is there to help them to discover the healing power of God's love to change whatever sin or sins they have fallen into.

B. Using the open question technique, discuss with individuals their experience of the reception of penance. Use questions such as:

- Have you ever celebrated this sacrament face-to-face? How was that experience different from the traditional form? Would you like to try going to confession in this way?
- Have you ever had a "special" experience of this sacrament?
- What do you remember about your first confession?
- How often do you celebrate this sacrament? Is going to confession something you do of your own free choice, or do your parents decide?
- What do you expect of the priest in this sacrament?
- Do you think this unit will make a difference in your attitude toward the sacrament?

C. Do not close this unit without setting up some kind of situation in which the students have a chance to go to confession. This can be done in several ways: set up a penance service at which many priests will be present, or arrange for each student to have a 10 minute appointment with the priest of his choice.

    Explain to the priests who take part in this reconciliation experience the main outline of the unit you have just completed with the students.

D. After the confession experience, give the students an opportunity to share their feelings about it. Was it a better experience than before? Did they find it helpful? Will they choose to do it again? Be sure to honor their pass privilege.

Session 10 — Sin as our parents understood it

A. Because the understanding of sin presented above is quite different from that once given to the students' parents, I find it helpful to give the class some understanding of how their parents would have been taught the same material we have just covered. To do this I distribute to the class copies of some pages of the Baltimore Catechism dealing with sin, and of the examination of conscience from an old missal. Have the students read the pages and comment or ask questions.

B. Give the students the list of questions below, and have them write short answers to them in their notebooks. Then tell them that their homework assignment is to discuss these same questions with their parents. The students should take notes on their parents' answers to the questions. In class the next day, discuss the parents' answers. How were they like, unlike, the students' answers? What is the reason for the difference? How did the parents, the students, feel about doing this exercise?

- What is a good person?
- How do you decide what is right and wrong?
- What is the purpose of the 10 Commandments?
- What is sin?
- What is the purpose of a list of sins in a prayerbook?
- What is the punishment for sin?
- What do you have to do to get rid of sin in your life?

Session 11 — Feedback

A. This could come at the end of the unit, or be interspersed at the ends of various lessons. Give the students unfinished sentences like:

- Now I understand. . . .
- I still don't see. . . .
- I think I will have a hard time. . . .
- I have definitely made up my mind to. . . .
- Someday I hope. . . .
- I wonder if. . . .

B. Share responses

C. Refer to the statements written the first day of the unit. Ask the class if the problems brought up that day have been resolved. If not, try to handle them now.

Session 12

A. Listed below are some typical comments of teenagers concerning sin and penance.

"The Commandments are just a bunch of old laws printed in the bible. They don't apply to modern man."

"How can a God who loves us punish us for every little sin?"

"If you think something isn't a sin, then it isn't a sin for you."

"It's easy to get rid of sin. God is so good, you just tell him you're sorry and he'll forgive you."

"I don't see why we have to go to confession. Why can't we just go straight to God?"

Ask the students to summarize this unit by writing a response to each of the above statements.

B. *Or* role play the statements. Have one student pose the question and another try to convince him of the answers we have been considering.

Unit 7

The Bible/Reading the Old Testament

This unit is intended to introduce adolescents to the bible, especially to the Old Testament. It was designed as a quarter course for freshmen, but it could be used with any group which has never really become acquainted with the bible. (It is not unusual to find teens who have never held a bible in their hands, who have never read from it, who have only a vague notion that it is a thick book full of rules.)

The unit teaches the students some basic facts about the bible and its place in history, has them handle the book so that they become familiar with its format and arrangement, and guides them through a reading of the stories of Abraham, Joseph and David, and of some of the non-story material in the Pentateuch and the Wisdom Books. All of this is meant simply to help the teens to discover what kind of book the bible is, what kind of material they can expect to find in it, and where.

The teacher's own attitude toward the bible will be a strong vehicle of communication during these sessions.

Session 1 — Finding your way around

A. Introduce the Values Voting strategy.[1] After several items from the book, give the following items about the bible. (Students answer questions by hand signals: yes—hand up, no—thumbs down, emphatic yes—hand up and waved around, emphatic no—thumbs down and teeth gritted.) After the show of hands on an individual item, call on a few students to explain the position they showed by their hand signal.

How many of you
- know how many books there are in the bible?
- think a unit on the bible will be boring?
- ever read a whole book of the bible?
- ever read a whole page of the bible?
- ever had to copy pages of the bible for a punishment?
- have a bible at home? one of your very own?
- pick it up and read from it sometimes? at least once a week?
- saw the movie "10 Commandments"? saw "Jesus of Nazareth" on TV?
- believe that what the bible says is always true?

[1]*Values Clarification*, p. 38.

89

B. Give out complete bibles. Call out the items listed below. The students should see who can find them fastest. Don't go on to the next item till all have found the last. Give brief explanations of each item once the students have opened the bible to it.

- The New Testament (Mention the relative proportion of the New Testament to the whole bible.)
- John's Gospel.
- Poems written by David (The book of Psalms is in the center of the book).
- The book of Genesis.
- Acts of the Apostles.
- A love story (Song of Songs).
- Story of Noah's Ark.
- A parable.
- The 10 Commandments (Exodus 20).
- A letter from Paul (Draw attention to the other letters also).
- The words: "Take and eat, this is my body" (Point out how to find parallel references.)

When you have been through all of these, repeat them, making a game of it by giving points to the first three finders each time.

C. Assignment: Select five people of different ages and different backgrounds, for example—your grandmother, a Protestant neighbor, a child, the bus driver, a friend your age. Ask each of these people what they think about the bible, whether they think it is all true, and how often they read it.

Write, for each of the five, a paragraph telling about the person and a summary of the discussion with him or her.

Session 2 — Naming the books

A. Discuss the responses to the homework assignment.

B. Turn to the table of contents of the Bible. Tell the students that you expect them to know for a test in the near future

1) The number of books in the Old Testament (45), New Testament (27), bible (72).
2) The kinds of books in the OT (Pentateuch, Historical books, Wisdom literature, Prophetic books).
3) The kinds of writing in the NT and the number of each kind of book (Gospels—4, Epistles—21, Acts—1, Revelation—1).
4) The names of the books of the Pentateuch (Genesis, Exodus, Leviticus, Numbers, Deuteronomy. Practice pronouncing them with the students.)
5) The names of 8 historical books (any eight).
6) The names of the major Prophets (Isaiah, Jeremiah, Ezekiel, Daniel. Practice pronouncing with the students.)
7) The names of the four Gospels (Matthew, Mark, Luke, John).
8) The names of the Epistle writers (Paul, James, Peter, John, Jude).
9) The languages in which the bible was first written (Greek, Hebrew, Aramaic).

C. Challenge the better students to learn the names of all 72 books.

Session 3 — Is the bible true?

A. Explain: The question "Is the bible true?" can be answered only if we realize that there are different kinds of truth.

- Scientific truth: The earth revolves around the sun.
- Geographical truth: Israel is northeast of Egypt.
- Historical truth: George Washington was our first president.
- Mathematical truth: 2+2=4
- Truth about relationships: My parents love each other.
- Truth about personalities: Sue is kind and friendly.
- Religious truth: God loves all people.
- Moral truth: Stealing is wrong.
- Proverbial truth: A stitch in time saves nine.
- Symbolic truth: Her eyes were dancing stars.

In each case above, you give the kind of truth (list on the board as you go along) and have the class give you examples. Discuss how each thing above is true and how each illustrates a different kind of truth.

B. What kinds of truth will we find in the bible? Have the class put a plus (+) in front of the kinds of truth that will be found there, and explain their choices. Put a double plus (+ +) in front of those they think the bible will be strongest on. Put a minus (−) in front of the kinds of truth the bible will be weakest on.

- Explain that the bible reflects the scientific understanding of the time it was written, so anything that has to do with science could be inaccurate.
- The geography in the bible is accurate as far as it goes, which isn't very far. Use a map to show the students the part of the world the bible writers were familiar with.
- The bible is full of history, but since much of the history was passed on by word of mouth before it was written down, the history is not always accurate. Contemporary historians are constantly being amazed at how much of the history is accurate, however.
- The bible is meant to be, and is, religious truth. It is the true story of a love relationship between God and his people—a very rocky love story with lots of ups and downs, lots of failures and fresh starts.
  In this sense, the bible is a true record of God's love for his people and of their constant failures in loving him.

C. Give out copies of the summary sheet shown on page 92. Go over the sheet with the students. Ask them to take it home and show it to their parents. The parents are asked to comment on the sheet and return it for the next class.

Is the bible true?

That question can only be answered if we understand that there are different kinds of truth.

RELIGIOUS TRUTH — The bible is primarily religious truth. Religion is concerned with man's relationship with God, and the bible is the record of the relationship between God and his chosen people, the Hebrews. It tells how God treated them and how they responded (or failed to respond) to him.

MORAL TRUTH — The bible also contains much moral truth. Moral truth tells us what is right and wrong, what we must do and how we must live if we want to be good people and close to God. However, the Old Testament reflects the morality of the Hebrew people, and their standards were very different from ours. For instance, according to Hebrew morality, if a person poked out your eye, you were permitted to poke out one of his, if he knocked out your tooth, you could knock out one of his. The New Testament tells us that Jesus expressly raised the moral standards. "It was said of old . . ., but I say to you. . . ."

SYMBOLIC TRUTH — Much of the truth in scripture is told in symbols, parables, myths and allegories. We have to read between the lines to discover the truth being presented. The story of the tree of good and evil is an example of such a symbol. There is truth there, but it is religious truth, not factual truth about apples and snakes.

PROVERBIAL TRUTH — Much of the bible, especially the Wisdom books, is the kind of folksy truth contained in proverbs, like: Do unto others as you would have others do unto you; A stitch in times saves nine.

HISTORICAL TRUTH — The bible contains the history of the Hebrew people from about 2000 BC to 100 AD. Though much of this history was passed down orally for generations before it was written, it is, nonetheless, surprisingly accurate. There are, however, some historical errors in the bible.

SCIENTIFIC TRUTH — The biblical writers reflect the scientific understandings of their day, which—we now know—were very primitive. For instance, the bible describes the earth as flat, says the sun stood still, says the world was created in seven days. We are able to read right through the scientific errors in the bible and find the religious truth the writer was trying to get across. There was no need for God to reveal a more accurate understanding of science to his people. Revelation is concerned with religious truth not scientific truth. The Hebrew people didn't have to know that the world was round in order to be close to God.

(To make copies of this page, use duplicate in tear-out section at back of book.)

Session 4 — Creation

A. To show how religious truth and scientific inaccuracy exist side by side in the scriptures, read the creation accounts in Genesis. As you read, draw on the board a diagram of what is happening in the story. Have the students draw the diagram in their notebooks.

Gn 1:1 Earth is a big lump of darkness surrounded by water; the Spirit hovers over it all.

1:6 God creates a great dome that pushes some of the water up. There are floodgates in the dome that God opens when he wants it to rain.

1:9 He gathers the water still on earth into one great sea in the middle of the earth. (What was the name of the sea in the middle of their world?)

1:11 Plants grow.

1:14 He creates the sun, moon, and stars and sets them in the dome.

1:20 Birds and fish are created.

1:24 He creates animals.

1:26 God creates man and woman in his image, to be masters of the earth.

B. Now make a list of all the religious truths that can be found in that short chapter.

- •God created the world.
- •Everything God made was good.
- •God created man and woman as equals.
- •He created man to be master of the earth.
- •He created man in his own image—with intellect and will.
- •The word of God has the power to do what it says. (Let there be....)
- •One day a week has been blessed and made holy.

C. There is a second creation account, beginning with Genesis 2:5. Explain to the class that this is a completely different story, an earlier story than the first one. There were two creation stories in the oral traditions, and rather than select one of them, the writer of Genesis put them both in his written account.

Read the second creation story, having the students point out as they go along all the ways it is different from the first. Read Genesis 2 and 3.

D. Now make a list of some of the religious truths contained in Genesis 2 and 3.

Man lives with the "breath" (life) of God.
God gives man rules about how to use the earth.
Man breaks the rules and is punished.
Man is tempted to go contrary to what God tells him.
The temptations of the devil are always lies.
Man feels ashamed when he disobeys God.
We always try to blame someone else for our sins.

E. Feedback starters:[2]

I was surprised to learn that...   Now I understand...
I always thought that...   I am puzzled about...

Write these phrases on the board. Ask the students to complete the sentences in their notebooks. Share the responses orally.

[2]*Values Clarification*, p. 163.

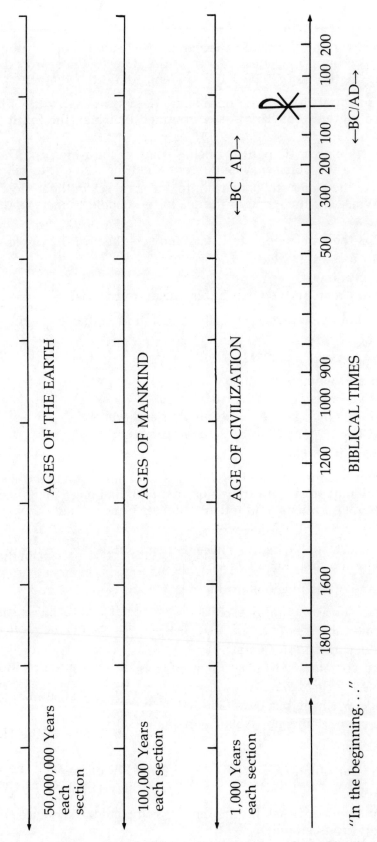

AGES OF THE EARTH

50,000,000 Years each section

AGES OF MANKIND

100,000 Years each section

AGE OF CIVILIZATION

←BC AD→

1,000 Years each section

BIBLICAL TIMES

←BC/AD→

200 100

100 200

300

500

900

1000

1200

1600

1800

"In the beginning..."

(To make copies of this page, use duplicate in tear-out section at back of book.)

Session 5 — Time line

A. Give out copies of the time line shown on page 94.

1) Explain that the first line represents the entire age of the earth. Each inch of that line represents 50,000,000 years. Where would they place man on the line? (Place man on the line about one-fourth inch from the right end.) Then space across the line such things as one-celled animals, invertebrates, dinosaurs, mammals, etc.

(The science does not have to be exactly accurate to get the idea across. If you want to be scientifically accurate, consult an encyclopedia.)

2) Now explain that we are going to take that last quarter inch, and stretch it out so we can see it better. The stretched-out quarter inch is our second line.

Notice that each division on this line is 100,000 years. Ask the students to tell what fraction of the line represents cavemen and what fraction represents civilized man. Again, civilized man is represented by a tiny fraction of the last inch to the right. Space across the line such things as stone age, fire, cave paintings, bows and arrows. (If you want to be really accurate, consult an encyclopedia for more detail.) Again we are going to take the last quarter inch and stretch it out to get line three.

3) Each division on line three represents 1000 years. Explain the position of Jesus on the line, and the division of time into AD and BC. Locate on the line such things as

1500 AD	Discovery of America
3000 BC	Egyptian and Babylonian civilizations
1000 BC	Greek civilization
500 BC	Roman civilization
500 AD+	European civilization
2000 BC	Hebrews
1200 BC	Alphabet invented
4000 BC	Wheel invented
3500 BC	Writing (picture writing)
6000 BC	Farming and villages first begun

4) Mark off on the time line the space between 2000 BC and 100 AD and explain that that is the period of time covered by the bible. That space of time is stretched out on the next line.

As you locate the following items on the biblical line, tell briefly the whole history of the Hebrew people. Have a map handy to point out where the events mentioned take place.

"In the beginning"—all the time before 1800 BC is lumped together in the bible under the phrase "in the beginning." This is only the first 15 or so pages of the Bible; it includes the creation stories, Adam and Eve, Cain and Abel, the tower of Babel, and Noah and the flood.

1800 BC Abraham, Isaac, and Jacob, the great patriarchs of the Hebrew nation.

1600 BC Joseph, the son of Jacob, sold into Egypt as a slave. The whole tribe of Jacob migrates to Egypt. Eventually it becomes enslaved there.

> 1200 BC Moses, called by God to lead the Hebrews out of slavery.
> 1200–1000 BC Judges, led the people in the fight for the promised land.
> 1000 BC Period of the great kingdom: Saul, David and Solomon.
> 900 BC The kingdom splits, the north is called Israel, the south Judah.
> 500 BC The nation is defeated by Babylon and taken into exile.
> 330 BC Alexander the Great conquers the known world.
> 200 BC Religious persecution of the Jews; the Maccabees revolt against their pagan leaders.
> 100 BC Rome conquers the known world.
> 39 BC to 39 AD The Herods reign as kings of Palestine.
> Christ is born.
> 33 AD Christ dies.
> 40–200 AD Christianity is spread to the whole Mediterranean world.

B. When was the bible written?

   1) The Old Testament was written over a long period of time, from the time of King Solomon, about 970 BC to about 150 BC. It includes also things that had been preserved in oral tradition from 1800–1000 BC.

   2) The New Testament was written from about 40 AD to about 150 AD.

Show these times on the time line so the students see the great contrast in the span of time covered by the OT and the NT. Discuss the significance of this difference.

C. Tell the class that you expect them to know all the material on these time lines for a test in the near future. For the test give them another blank time line paper and ask them to fill in the items given.

Reading Sessions

Spend many sessions simply reading together from the scriptures. Call on volunteers to read orally, or you yourself read. If you have read the section ahead of time in a good commentary, you will have interesting bits of explanation to intersperse with the readings. In reading a story from scripture, skip over genealogies and other such sections that do not move the story forward.

Some suggested Old Testament readings are listed below:
The story of Abraham—Gen. 12, 15, 16–19, 21–22
Isaac and Jacob—Gen. 25, 27–35
The story of Joseph—Gen. 37, 39–45
The story of Moses—Ex.1–6:13, 7–11, 12:21–41, 13:17–22, 14, 15:19–27, 16–20, 24, 32–34:9, 34:27–35, 40:16–38
To give the class a flavor of some of the non-story material in the Pentateuch read:
Lev. 19–20; 24:17–22
Num. 1; 6:22; 31:1–24
Deut. 4:7–20; 5:1–22; 6:4–9; 13:7–11; 21:18–21; 27:15–27; 30:11–20
Samson: Judges 13–16
Samuel and David: 1 Sam 16–19
2 Sam 11–13
Solomon: 1 Kings 3: 1–28, 10:14–11:13

Fall of Jerusalem: Jeremiah 52:4-16
                     Baruch 6:1-6
Maccabean revolt: Maccabees 6-7

The above readings will give your class a sense of the main historical events presented on the time line. Also, select sections of Psalms and the Wisdom books to read, discuss, and pray over.

Project Sessions

Intersperse the reading sessions with projects such as these:

1) Show a filmstrip[3] about a section you have just read. Compare the film with the scriptural account.
2) Have the students dramatize a particular reading, e.g., the Joseph story.
3) Have the students create a booklet in which they select and illustrate passages from the Wisdom literature. (Five passages each from Proverbs and Wisdom. Ten passages each from Sirach and Psalms.) Show them how to write biblical reference notes—e.g.: Ps. 84:5-6
4) Discuss some of the real-life situations of sinfulness found in the OT stories they have read. Why are such stories found in the bible?
5) Have the students make a list of OT readings that would be appropriate to use in liturgies with teens.

[3]ROA films.

Unit 8

Jesus and the New Testament

This unit introduces the students to our chief source of knowledge about Jesus, the New Testament.

The unit first helps the students to locate Jesus

a) in history—Jesus of Nazareth was a flesh and blood person who lived on earth at a specific time and in a specific place, b) in theology and doctrine—Jesus is the Christ, the Second Person of the Blessed Trinity who "became flesh and dwelt among us."

The unit then attempts to give the students a sense of the New Testament: where did these writings come from? who were the people who wrote them? what were they trying to say? how dependable are they as sources of knowledge about Jesus? The presentation answers these questions using broad strokes, emphasizing the closeness of the 27 documents to the Christ event. Details of scriptural scholarship are used sparingly and loosely to fill in the overall sketch.[1]

This unit could be used as an introduction to a longer study of Jesus or the New Testament. It could also be combined with Unit 7 to form an introductory course on the bible. If the units are combined, take session 1 of Unit 8 before session 5 of Unit 7.

Session 1 — Jesus and God

A. Ask the students a series of questions designed to bring out into the open the confusion in their minds concerning the relationship between Jesus and God. Ask each question of several different students. Ask if they agree with each other's answers, and if the answers make sense in relationship to one another.

- Are Jesus and God the same person?
- Do you pray to God or to Jesus?
- Is Jesus the Son of God in the same way that you are the son or daughter of your father?
- Did Jesus create the world?
- Did God die on the cross?
- Is Jesus alive or dead right now? Was he dead at one time?
- Is Jesus God? Who did he talk to when he prayed? Himself?
- Can you call yourself a Christian if you don't think Jesus is God?

[1] I am aware that the explanation of the New Testament offered here is open to the charge of oversimplification. I am convinced, however, that this simplified presentation is justified by my primary intention: to build in the teens a positive attitude toward the New Testament as a reliable source of Christian truth. In my experience, too much technical detail too soon confuses adolescents, sometimes even destroying their faith in the New Testament itself and their interest in further study of it.

B. Tell the students, now that they are all thoroughly confused, that you will try to clarify for them the relationship between Jesus and God.

Explain that there once was an actual historical person named Jesus who lived and died in a little country on the eastern shores of the Mediterranean Sea. (Point it out on a map.) How long ago did that person live? Where would he fit in history with other historical figures they might know about? To answer these questions, draw a line across the board. Tell them that the left end of the line represents the beginning of the world, and the right end represents the present year. Ask them to tell you where on the time line they would place the man Jesus who once lived in the country of Palestine. Have students come to the board and place an X on the line to represent when they think Jesus lived. The X's will be all over the line.) After several students have offered guesses, put 1000-year division lines a short space apart starting from the right. Can they tell you now more precisely where to place Jesus? (Some bright student might know that Jesus lived exactly 1978 years ago.) Tell them that Jesus actually lived a little less than 2000 years ago. Place a Chi Rho on the line, two 1000-year spaces from the right. (Explain that the Chi Rho is a symbol made from two Greek letters—the first two letters in the Greek spelling of Christ, χριστο.)

Actually the line above is still not properly proportioned. The time before Christ is much longer. But this will be sufficient to get the point across. To help the students to see the proper perspective, locate a few other events on the time line: 1500 AD, discovery of America; 3000 BC, the great Egyptian civilization and the Babylonians; 1000 BC, the Greek civilization; 500 BC, the Romans; about 5000 BC, invention of the wheel and writing; about 7000 BC, the beginning of farming; somewhere before that the stone age and iron age; before that, the age of dinosaurs. (This is very sketchy history. If you want to make it more exact, an encyclopedia will give you the latest facts and figures.) Have the students name some other great historical figures and show where they would be located on the time line.

C. Now ask the students to locate <u>God</u> on the time line. Give them a few tries, then explain that since God is before all time and after all time and above and beyond and through all time, we will use an infinite triangle located above our time line to stand for him. Have students explain why we use a triangle to stand for God, and label the three corners of the triangle.

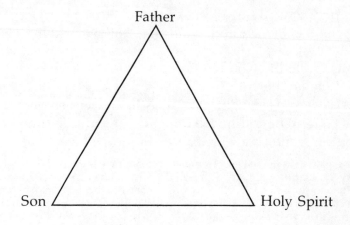

D. Now ask: What is the relationship between this eternal, invisible, three-personed God and the human being named Jesus who lived 2000 years ago on the eastern shore of the Mediterranean Sea? Draw out the answer from the class, or explain:

The man Jesus and the second person of the Blessed Trinity (the Son) are the same person. This is the mystery of the INCARNATION. This is difficult material to understand. Tell the students that no human person will ever fully understand it, because we are dealing with the two great mysteries of Christianity:

  a) Trinity: There are three persons in one God—God the Father, God the Son and God the Holy Spirit.

  b) Incarnation: Jesus Christ is the Second Person of the Trinity. Jesus is really God and really man.

E. Explain that many of the major heresies over the 2000 years of Christianity have concerned that mystery. In trying to explain how Jesus could be both God and man, some people have leaned too far toward the man end of the spectrum, others have leaned too far toward the God end. Either is heresy. The true teaching is that he is at the same time God and man. Ask the students to try to locate their ideas of Jesus on the spectrum. Do they think of him as more God or more man? Where would they locate the teaching they got in grade school? from their parents? Where would "Jesus Christ Superstar" and "Godspell" fit?

```
                          GOD
                          AND
MAN                       MAN
                                                    GOD
<———————————————————————————————————————————————————————>
ONLY                                                ONLY
                  TRUE CHRISTIAN DOCTRINE
Heresy
                                                    Heresy
```

F. Return to the questions asked in A above. Help the students to answer them in terms of the lesson you have just taught. Assign the questions for homework.

Session 2 — What is the New Testament?

A. Pass out copies of the New Testament. Ask the students: if we were to find this book in its original form, what would it look like? Where would you go to look for the original? What languages would we find it in? Then explain:

During the first 100 years after Jesus died many things were written about him by people who knew him or knew his apostles. Many of these earliest writings have been lost. But we still have *27 old documents* that everyone agrees are authentic records of the earliest years of the church of Jesus. Unfortunately, we do not have the original copy of any of these documents, but we do have several very early copies of the originals. By comparing these, historians can tell what the originals would have said.

In their original form these 27 ancient documents would have been parchment scrolls, written in Hebrew or Greek or Aramaic. They were the work of persons who made up the early Christian communities in many of the countries on the shores of the Mediterranean: Asia Minor, Palestine, Greece, Rome, Egypt (show on map.) You have in your hands a translation of those 27 documents. The translation was made recently by a group of scholars who went back to the oldest documents and translated directly from the Hebrew or Greek into modern English. (Compare this to the older bibles which were three times removed from the originals, since they had been translated from Greek to Latin and from Latin to English.)

B. Now let's look at what kind of documents these are. (List the kinds at the board.)

1) Most of them are *letters*. After Jesus' death the apostles traveled around the Mediterranean area teaching. They would establish a Christian community in one town, then move on to another. Many of the letters were written to one of the communities, some to individual persons in them. Sometimes the letters are encouragement, sometimes scoldings, sometimes explanations of a point of doctrine. Let's look at some samples. (Have the students open to Paul's letter to Philemon. Read it to them.)

Suppose we had salvaged only this old document from the Jesus years. What would we know about him? What would we know about the writer, Paul? The receiver, Philemon?

Read Romans 16 as another example of Paul's letter writing.

2) Four of the ancient documents are *Gospels*. The Gospels are something like *memoirs*. (Have the students explain what memoirs are, who writes them, why?) Those who knew Jesus wrote their memories of him and of the experience of belonging to the group who loved him. If four people wrote their memoirs of the same man, John F. Kennedy, how would the four compare?

The Gospels were written by people who heard the teaching of Jesus, who saw him die, and who experienced his resurrection. The resurrection is the event that colors everything they think and say about him. The Jesus they are telling about is still alive, still very much with them. Even though they saw him die, they continue to experience his living presence and power. It is this living Lord, not a dead man, whose life and teaching is recorded in the Gospels. Have the students open to Matthew and skim through it, looking at chapter heads. Then turn to Mark and read the first line. Explain that *Good News* is the meaning of "gospel." Skim through Mark. Then turn to Luke. Read the first four verses carefully. These explain what the Gospel writers were trying to do: give an orderly account of the life of Jesus as it was told by those who "saw these things from the beginning." Skim through Luke and John.

3) One of the ancient documents is something like a *diary*. Turn to *Acts*. Point out the similarity to the beginning of Luke—this is Luke's second book, in which he records the things that happened after Jesus' ascension. Skim through the book, explaining that most of it is a record of Paul's missionary journeys. Notice that, starting with Chapter 20, Luke shifts to first person. (We sailed, we spent a week.) During this part of the journey he seems to be traveling with Paul.

4) The last document is strange, exotic *poetry* written by John. Much of it has never been fully understood. Skim *Revelation*. Read 1:9–20, 5:6–8, 12:1–9.

D. From what we've said so far, do you think you can read these documents as reliable sources? Either discuss this answer or have students write about it.

Session 3 — When was the New Testament written?

A. When were these documents written? Present the time line below, explaining that it is approximate, not exact. Early writers did not date their writings as we do today, so scholars have to go by internal evidence—historical events and people that are mentioned—to date the books.

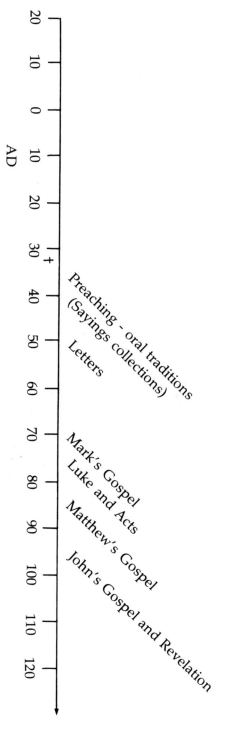

1) Preaching and oral tradition

The first teaching about Jesus was oral. Soon after the resurrection the apostles began to gather people together to tell them who Jesus was and what his life meant to them. An example of one of these early sermons is found in Acts 2. (Read with class Acts 2:14–17, 22–24, 29–38.) The preaching of the apostles, repeated over and over to group after group, is known as the oral tradition. (Ask the students if they have heard their parents or grandparents telling about events from their youth or childhood. Have they heard the same story told many times? From different points of view? How true are these stories to the original event?)

2) Collections of sayings

Eventually people began writing down some of the words and deeds of Jesus. Collections of the sayings of Jesus and of his miracle stories were made and passed around. The original copies of these collections have all been lost, but scripture scholars can locate traces of them in the Gospels. The Gospel writers used such written accounts when writing their own Gospels. (Refer again to Luke 1:1–4. Luke says he is pulling together many things that have been written about Jesus.)

3) Letters

The earliest written materials we have are the missionary letters of the apostles, which some scholars date as early as 50 AD. Paul would start a Christian community in one city, then move on to another. He kept in touch with each group by mail—writing letters to encourage the Christian communities, to answer questions about the faith, and sometimes to scold them. Twenty-one of the documents in the New Testament are letters like this. How dependable would you say these are as sources for discovering what the early church believed and taught?

4) The Gospels

The earliest Gospel, Mark's, was probably written about 70 AD. Matthew and Luke both seem to have used Mark's Gospel when writing their own, keeping some of his ideas and changing others. John's Gospel was written many years later and is very much different from the other three. We are not sure that Matthew, Mark, Luke and John actually are the persons who wrote these Gospels. It is more likely that each Gospel is the product of the community of Christians started by these men. So we would have the Gospel as it was preached by each man to his community.

B. Feedback session. Have the students write completions for the sentence starters listed below. Discuss the responses.

The thing that most surprised me in this lesson was. . . .

I am confused about. . . .

The part of the New Testament I would like to read is. . . .

I wonder why. . . .

Session 4 — What the New Testament says

A. When we read through these old documents there are two separate questions we are concerned about: What do they say about the early Christians' experience of Jesus? What do they say to _me_ (or do _I_ believe what they say?) This lesson concerns only the first question: What do the New Testament writings say about Jesus?

B. Now tell the story of Jesus in such a way that you involve your students in the story. Substitute towns they know for biblical towns, talk to them as if they are the apostles, the blind beggars, the prostitutes, etc.

> We all live 2000 years ago in a little country in Palestine. We're simple people, quite poor; John here is the only one in town who can read. We hear that there's this young prophet from Podunk (substitute a very small "hick" town near you) who's been causing quite a stir down in Madison (substitute a big city near you.) Peggy (one of the students in your class) heard from her Aunt Susan who heard from her neighbor that this prophet is actually supposed to have turned water into wine. Peggy doesn't believe it, of course, but she has told everyone in town. And Bill (you are looking at Bill, of course) has a cousin who has a friend in Madison. Now his friend's brother has been lame from birth, and Bill heard yesterday that the young prophet, his name is Jesus isn't it? anyway Bill heard that the prophet touched his friend's friend's brother's leg, and he can walk. And _we_ hear that Jesus is coming to Springfield! How will you react? What will you do? Say?
>
> Over a period of three years, these are some of the things we learn about the man named Jesus. Some we see ourselves, others we hear about. (List the key things at the board as you talk. Keep the story alive. Bring your students in as your examples.)
>
> a) Jesus has a powerful effect on people:
>   - Andrew quit his job as a fisherman to be with him.
>   - Barney, who was blind from birth, can see now because of him.
>   - Maggy—we all know what kind of girl she was—has stopped chasing around so she can follow him.
>
> b) Jesus teaches about God in a new and exciting way:
>   - He always calls God "Abba," which is like our word "Daddy."
>   - He says we should love our enemies, forgive those who wrong us, and give everything away for love of others.
>   - He claims to be starting a new kingdom. (What kind of king would come from Podunk!?)
>
> c) Jesus has a lot of enemies. The authorities in Madison are out to get him. We wake up one morning to hear he has been arrested. By noon of that same day we see him executed as a criminal. All his friends, including us, have deserted him. Discuss with the class how we would have felt that day: angry, betrayed, doubting, afraid. Do we still believe all those things he said about starting a kingdom and being the Son of God?
>
> d) Then comes the strangest experience of all. We who saw Jesus die know that he is alive again. Lucy saw the empty tomb. Mike talked to him. Tom actually put his finger in the hole in his hand. Leo and Barry had supper with him. That is the experience that changes our lives. Jesus is alive! We are so excited by this experience that we spend the rest of our lives telling people about it.

e) We spread out all over Wisconsin (your state) telling everyone we meet about Jesus and forming little groups of people who are willing to live according to his teachings. Whenever we get together we try to refresh our memories about the things he said and did. When a problem comes up, we try to solve it in the light of his teachings. What will we do if someone starts mixing up the message of Jesus? How much chance is there that any real errors will creep into our teaching? Supposing you learn, Judy, that Tom says there were three blind men cured near Burlington and you know there were only two? (Probably nothing. No big problem.) Supposing you learn that Larry is teaching that only people with Irish blood can belong to the Kingdom? (This is one of the big problems that the Apostles had to fight out among themselves: was the teaching of Jesus for everyone or only for the Jewish people?)

Paul is our most avid missionary. Within 20 years he has established a Christian community in Menasha, Oshkosh, Green Bay, and all the way across the state to Eau Claire and Chippewa. He even sails across Lake Michigan (gets shipwrecked on the way!) to bring the good news to Grand Rapids and Detroit. And Paul keeps writing letters to the churches he starts. (Substitute cities in your state.) Finally, about 40 years after Jesus' death, the people in Mark's church over in LaCrosse decide to write down the whole story of Jesus' life, death, and resurrection. A few years later, Luke's church up in Adams also writes about Jesus. So do John's church in Kenosha and Matthew's church in Appleton. If you got all four of these accounts side by side, how would you expect them to compare to one another?

C. Two thousand years from now a group of sophomores will be reading our letters and memoirs and trying to find out something about this man named Jesus. Do you think they will believe what we have written? What will make it extra hard? What will make it easier?

Session 5 — Can I believe what the New Testament says?

A. Have the students look up the story of the cure of two blind men: Matt 20:29–34. Show them how to use the footnotes to find the parallel references: Mark 10: 46–52 and Luke 18:35–43. Discuss the minor differences in the three and ask the students how they would account for them.

B. Now for the question: Why did these men write this story? Suggest four possible answers, all of which have been given by various people over the years.

a) They are simply telling about a historical event, a fact of history. It really happened as they recorded it here.

b) They are lying. They are making up a story in order to deceive people, to make Jesus look greater than he really was.

c) They have been tricked into believing it happened. Jesus was a magician or a sorcerer who had his disciples duped into believing what isn't really true.

d) They are talking in symbolic language. It was the man's inner spiritual blindness that was cured, and the gospel writers describe the cure in terms of physical blindness.

Have each student indicate by raising his hand which of the four he thinks it is. Call on individuals to give reasons for their choices. At this stage most of your class will opt for (a) or (d) or a combination of those two. Have the students explain why they think it isn't (b) or (c). (In discussing (b) it is interesting to point out what the apostles "got" for teaching this: torture, jail, death.)

C. Look up various accounts of the resurrection: Matt 28:1–15, Mark 16:1–8, Luke 24:1–12; Romans 6:4–9; Acts 2:23–24, 32–36.

Apply the four answers above to these accounts, also. (Some of your students may have heard or read about the *Passover Plot*, a book which says the resurrection was a hoax. If the question comes up, tell them that it is not a new question, but has been around for 2000 years. Refer them to Matt 28:11–15.)

D. The big question is still: Do I believe what is written in this book? If there are still many nonbelievers in the group, have a debate on the credibility of the book: To Believe or Not to Believe.

Or simply have the students answer the question, giving all the reasons they can for their answer.

Session 6 — The miracles of Jesus
_____

A. Clarify the use of the words "external change" and "internal change"

   —external: making blind eyes see
              calming a stormy sea
              healing a leper
   —internal: making a "blind" person see the truth
              calming a disturbed life
              healing a person who is rotten inside

Discuss: Which would be the greater miracle, an external change or an internal change? Which would you rather have happen to you? Which would Jesus be more concerned about doing? Which did he do?

B. Possibilities concerning the miracles related in scripture:

   a) They are feats of *magic*. This is an idea Jesus himself and the Gospel writers are always trying to correct. Magic was a big part of the world of the ancient peoples. The large crowds who followed Jesus were looking for magic tricks. Help the class to see that there is no love in magic. The magician uses his special powers to trick and deceive, to get attention for himself, not to show love to someone else. Jesus did not want followers who wanted to be entertained by magic tricks.

   b) They are *acts of personal kindness*. Jesus is using his divine power to help an individual person in need. This would seem to be a plausible answer, but then the problem arises: why didn't he cure every blind person, every lame person? Why didn't he wipe out all the sickness and misery on the earth? If the power of God could do these things, why doesn't it?

   c) The miracles are *signs*. The curing of a blind man is a sign of the power of God's love to cure the blindness in men's hearts. Changing water into wine is a sign of the transformation that takes place in the life of one who lets God's love touch him.

Discuss: Which of these three options would you say best fits the miracles in scripture? Explain: The miracles in scripture are explicity called "signs." See John 2:1–11, 4:54, 20:30–31.

C. Assuming the miracles are signs, there are still two possibilities concerning the miracles related in scripture.

    a) Jesus actually brought about an external change (eg. making a blind person see) as a *sign* of an internal personal change that was happening in the man's heart. ("That you may know that the son of man has power on earth to forgive sins. Then he said to the paralytic, 'Stand up, take up your bed, and walk.'")

    b) The New Testament tells the story of an external change as a way of describing a mysteriously wonderful internal change. This would be symbolic truth, not falsehood.

We do not know if an individual miracle related in scripture is (a) or (b). In some cases it seems Jesus actually brought about a miraculous external change; in some cases it seems more likely that the Gospel writer is telling about a mysterious and powerful internal change *by* describing an external change. The important thing is not whether an individual miracle story portrays symbolic truth or straight historical fact. (See unit 7, session 5). It might be either. Jesus *could* have done all the things the Gospels say he did. But what is really important is the *why* of the miracle stories as reported by scripture. What does this miracle story tell us about this person, Jesus, who is God living among us? What does it mean to *me* that the Jesus of Scripture gives life to a little girl, cures lepers, feeds 5000 hungry people, walks on water, etc.? What do these miracles tell me about *God and about my relationship to him?*

D. Read the following miracle accounts and discuss them in light of the above.

Cana—John 2:1–12	Bread—Matt 16:8–11
Official's son—John 4:43–54	Leper—Mark 1:40–45
Blind man—John 9:1–7, 35–39	Paralyzed man—Luke 5:17–25
Lazarus—John 11:1–44	Storm—Luke 8:22–25
Walking on water—John 6:16–21	Jarius' daughter—Luke 8:40–56

E. Write an essay developing this topic sentence: The miracles of Jesus are signs of God's love for all men, and of the power of his love to change the life of any man who will accept it.

Session 7 — Interviewed by Jesus

A. Tell the class that you are going to have a guest today who is going to ask them some questions. You're going to be leaving, but he'll be here in a few minutes. Go out the door, and come back in, impersonating Jesus. Introduce yourself as Jesus of Nazareth. Go from student to student asking them the questions listed below. (Don't be bound by these, of course. Use them as guides for your own creativity.)

- What's your name? Are you glad you came to class today?
- What do you think is the biggest problem in the world? What are you doing to solve it? Is there something you think I should do about it?
- How well do you know my Father? Have my followers done a good job of telling you about him?
- What would you like me to do for your family? for you? your friends?
- Do you think your religion classes have helped or hindered your love for me?
- What do you think about my church? Do you think it's going the way I planned?
- How would you suggest it be improved?
- Are you afraid to die? What do you think will happen after death? Do you believe in Hell?

- Do you know anyone who really lives the way I expect people to live? Tell me about him. Would you like to live that way? What seems to be the biggest obstacle?
- Can I come to your house for supper? How will you introduce me? Do you think the supper table will be different because I am there?
- Would you introduce me to your girl (boy) friend? How would you explain who I am? If I spent an evening with the two of you would I spoil your fun?
- Can I spend the whole day with you tomorrow? How do you think the day will go with me along? How would you explain me to your friends?
- What do you think of (teacher's name)'s classes? Do you think the discussions are clearing up your problems about me or making them worse? What should I tell him/her to do to improve?
- Are you usually happy? What do you need to make you happier than you are?
- Perfectly happy?
- Would you like to be my friend? I seem to have trouble making friends in this school. What do you think is my problem?

B. Tell the class you have enjoyed chatting with them. Say good-by, and leave. Come back in as just your little old self. Ask the class how they enjoyed their guest. Would they like him to come again?

Session 8 — Interviewing Jesus

Follow the same strategy as last session, only this time the students get to ask Jesus the questions. Good luck in answering them!

Session 9 — Bringing the scriptures to life

A. Read or tell the story of the woman caught in adultery. (John 8)

B. Divide the class up so that each has a part in the story: the woman, Jesus, the friends of Jesus, the Pharisees, the woman's husband, her lover's wife, curious on-lookers. You take the role of a news reporter and interview everybody. (If you have journalism students in the class, they could do the interviewing. They would have to prepare their questions ahead of time. So would you, of course.)

C. Have each person give his judgment as to whether the woman should be stoned or not. She is definitely guilty—she was caught in the act. The law says she should be stoned. Judgment should be given according to the role each is playing.

D. Ask the students to write the thoughts that went through the woman's mind

When she was caught.   While Jesus was writing in the sand.
When she was thrown at Jesus' feet.   When she finds herself alone with Jesus.

E. Discuss: Do you think she obeyed the words of Jesus: "Go and sin no more"?
   Note: Similar lessons could be prepared for many other New Testament stories. Many good ideas, such as this, for bringing New Testament readings to life can be found in the *Serendipity Books* by Lyman Coleman (Creative Resources, Waco, Texas.)

Session 10 — Parable of the Sower

A. Read the parable—Mark 4:1–9, 13–20

B. Give out duplicates of p. 110. Have students fill them in prayerfully and seriously.

C. Discuss the answers, using the open-question technique.

PARABLE OF THE SOWER   Mark 4:1–9, 13–20

A man went out to plant his seed...	Name the "sowers" in your life—the persons who have planted the Word of God in your soil.	Some seed fell on the path—the birds ate it before it ever sprouted...	In your life, who or what are the "birds" that snatch the seed of God away before it gets a chance?
Some fell on rocky ground. The soil wasn't deep enough—the plants soon dried up...	What might cause a person to be rocky soil—one who hears the word, begins to practice it, but soon gives up?	Some fell among thorns which grew up and choked the plants.	What are the thorns in your life—the worries or desires or riches that grow with the seed and crowd Christ out?

Some fell in good ground.   What definite things could you do each day to keep the seeds of Christianity growing and yielding fruit in your life? List 5.

Put a star next to the one of these things that you have definitely decided you will do.

JESUS PRESENTS A CONTINUUM IN THIS PARABLE. CAN YOU PLACE YOUR-SELF ON IT?

X	X	X	X	X	X
hardened ground—no growth	thin soil no roots— growth doesn't last	rich soil— but too many weeds	30-fold	60-fold	100-fold

(To make copies of this page, use duplicate in tear-out section at back of book.)

Unit 9

Sexuality/Love, Luv and Friendship

This unit is intended to help adolescents to understand sexuality as an important aspect of their total lives as Christian persons.

The lessons discuss sex a) as a physical, biological act, b) as a means of communication between human persons, and c) as a sacrament. In these sessions the adolescents are helped to understand the various kinds of love relationships they will experience in life, and are given a basis on which to make decisions concerning their own sexual conduct.

Session 1 — Where we are

A. Give the class an anonymous questionnaire to determine what previous teaching they have had concerning sexuality. The questions can be duplicated or given orally. I usually give them orally to get the class accustomed to the idea that I am not squeamish about sexual words and ideas.

Questionnaire:

Do not put your name on this paper. Simply indicate male or female at the top of the page.
1. Do you feel you have an adequate understanding of the act of intercourse, the act by which a man and woman cooperate to produce a child?
2. Do you have an adequate understanding of the reproductive system in the male body and how it works?
3. Do you have an adequate understanding of the reproductive system in the female body and how it works?
4. From whom did you learn what you now know about sex?
5. When you have questions on sex, whom do you ask?
6. How do you feel about a unit on sexuality taught by me in a mixed group?
7. How much do you and your friends "talk sex?"
8. What ideas, problems, do you think we should cover in this unit on sexuality?

B. I collect the papers and read the answers to the class. I usually read the first three answers together (yes, yes, no; yes, no, no). (You and the class will probably be surprised at the number of no's in the pack. I tell them if there were only one "no" in the whole pack I would see that as reason enough to go ahead with the unit.) Then I read all the answers to number 4, then all answers to number 5, and so on.

C. Ask the students to tell you about sex education classes they have had. Call on representatives from the various schools they have come from.

D. Explain to the class that we can talk about sex on three levels:

Physical—Sex on this level is a bodily function; it is the means of reproduction and a source of pleasure. Actually the understanding of sex on this level should be learned in biology classes, but just in case someone has not learned it, we will spend one session on it.

Personal—Sex on this level is a means of communication. It is one of the ways human beings express their feelings to one another. Most of this unit will be concerned with this aspect of sexuality.

Sacramental—Sex on this level is a sacrament. It is one of the means by which God's love in us grows. (This will surprise your students. They have probably never been told that sexual intercourse itself, if properly motivated, is sacramental.)

Session 2 — Physical level

Note: You could bring in a nurse or doctor to present this lesson. Or you could find a movie or filmstrip that would present the material thoroughly. I find that presenting it myself, with my simple drawings and diagrams, shows the class that I am not afraid of the subject, that I do consider sex holy. I also find that once we have broken the barrier on this subject, the students are freer in discussing other problem areas in their lives.

A. Have available a set of simple diagrams showing the male and female sexual organs. My set are handmade transparencies. Simply and directly teach the following terminology, explaining what each term means and its function in the reproductive process. Keep in mind that there are students who answered "no" to your first three questions, but the others will also be listening hard. Have the class take notes as you teach.

- Units of reproduction: egg and seed, or ovum and sperm
- Female body: womb or uterus, vagina, ovaries, fallopian tubes
- Male body: penis, testicles, semen, erection
- Sexual intercourse: the penis is placed in the vagina, sperm is ejaculated
- Fertilization: one sperm finds the ovum, penetrates it; conception
- Pregnancy: gestation, embryo, fetus, umbilical cord
- Birth: labor pains, dilation, placenta

Explain menstruation: what happens and why. Point out to the boys the necessity of understanding this phenomenon if they are to be sympathetic and respectful of the women in their lives—their mothers, sisters, girl friends. Explain nocturnal emissions or wet dreams. Point out to the girls the possibility of causing sexual discomfort to a boy by dressing or acting seductively.

B. Sexual pleasure

Explain simply that sexual pleasure is a very special kind of feeling. Teach the term orgasm. Explain that sexual pleasure comes faster for a man, that the act of intercourse can be distasteful, even painful, to a woman unless her husband is gentle and considerate, that a man must learn to perform the act so that it gives pleasure to his wife and not just to himself.

C. Sexual sins

Explain that sex is sinful when it does not respect the persons involved or the laws of God. Sex only for pleasure never satisfies; it eventually leads to self-disgust and destroys the dignity of those involved. Explain the following: fornication, adultery, double adultery, prostitution, homosexuality, masturbation.

D. Birth control

Explain that there are good reasons and bad reasons for wanting to control the size of one's family. Good reasons: to space children, to limit the number of children to the ability of the parents to care for them, to preserve the health of the mother. Bad reasons: to avoid the responsibility of children, to have more money for cars, boats and snowmobiles.

Explain simply the following methods of birth prevention. Point out on your diagrams how each works:

- Medicinal: pill
- Mechanical: foams, IUD, diaphragm, condum
- Natural: abstention, rhythm, Billings, sympto-thermic
- Permanent: vasectomy, tubal ligation
- Abortion

Point out that only the natural methods have been officially accepted by the church. Also indicate some of the other reasons against using the other methods: for example, some are not dependable, some endanger health, some are too much bother, some are abortive.

E. Pass out small pieces of paper. Ask the students to write on the paper: 1) a response to today's class, and 2) any questions they have about the material presented today. The papers are anonymous. Have the students fold the papers once and bring them up to you. When all papers are collected, shuffle them conspicuously before looking at them. Invite the students to stand and talk while you are looking over the papers. When you have reassembled the group, read the responses and questions to the class. If you do not have time to answer the questions, begin the next lesson by doing so.

Session 3 —Personal level

A. Tell the class that you are going to be explaining to them four kinds of relationships and some combinations of the four. Space across the top of the board:

(A) EXPLOITATION   (B) LUV   (C) FRIENDSHIP   (D) LOVE

As you describe the characteristics of each, list them under the titles. As much as possible draw the information out of the class.

(A) Begin with exploitation. Have the students tell you what it means to be "used." What are the ways in which people use one another? (Sex is only one way of using. Others include: car rides, copying homework, getting back at someone.) How do we feel when we realize that we have been used? How do girls use each other? How do boys use each other? How do boys use girls? Girls use boys?

(C) Skip next to friendship. Make it clear that you are talking about any kind of friendship: girl-girl, boy-boy, girl-boy, teen-adult. What characterizes friendship? List such things as: fun, respect, sharing, trust, understanding, lasting, non-exclusive.

(B) Take luv next. Explain that you are using that word to stand for the state of *being in love*. What is it like to be in love? How is it different from friendship? List such characteristics of luv as: extremes of happiness or dejection, always on your mind, jealousy, exclusive, physical, always together, loss of appetite, can't think of anything else.

(D) Now discuss love. What does it mean to really *love* someone? Again you are talking about love between any two persons. The discussion should bring out such key concepts as: real commitment, self-sacrifice, depth of understanding, great trust, lasts forever, deep mutual respect, willingness to forgive. Point out that love is the superlative of *friendship*, not of luv. This is a very important concept to get across to the teens.

B. Now apply the above to high school relationships. Most of them are combinations of the above. (Use large and small letters to indicate the type of relationship. E.g., a (Bc) relationship would be more luv than friendship, a (bC) relationship would be more friendship than luv, a (BC) relationship would be about equal parts friendship and luv.)

Ask the class to describe various relationships: (Ac), (aB), (Bc), (bC), (bD), etc.

Which would be more likely to get into sexual trouble, (Bc) or (bC) and why?

Discuss the various relationships in terms of marriage. Ideally which kind of relationship would be the best preparation for marriage? (Marriage itself is a lifetime of working out a BD relationship. It develops best from a bC relationship, since it is C (friendship) that matures into love.) What happens to a marriage that is based on a (Bc) relationship? An (aB) relationship? Point out that it is difficult to tell the difference between (B) and (D) when one is in the relationship, but in the long run B does not last. It cannot sustain the difficulties and problems of married life. Only D can do that, and it takes a lifetime to develop a D relationship.

C. The distinction between luv and love is crucial. One can live a happy, fulfilled life without luv, but no one can survive as a whole person without love. Love, not luv, makes the world go round. Luv happens; love must be worked at. Luv dies; love can live through the most difficult of circumstances. Luv can enhance love, but it can also destroy it. An interesting way of bringing home to your class the difference between love and luv might be a study of popular love songs. Have them bring their favorites to class, really listen to the words, and decide if the song is singing about love or luv.

D. Ask the students to think about boy-girl relationships they have had in the past. Tell them it is easier to tell just what kind of relationship one is involved in two or three years after it is over. Why?

1) Write down the names of all the girls (guys) you have had some kind of relationship with since seventh grade. Next to each write the kind of relationship you now think it was, using the letter combinations in B above. (These lists will *not* be shared.)

2) Write down the names of all the people in your life whom you really love. Those who really love you.

E. At the close of the lesson again give out slips of paper for responses and questions. (See E in Session 2.)

Session 4 — How far can we go?

A. When teens ask "How far can we go?" they mean how far can they progress along the continuum charted below without getting into trouble. Put the continuum on the board and explain the steps in it.

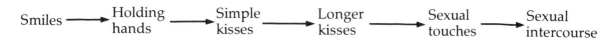

Smiles ⟶ Holding hands ⟶ Simple kisses ⟶ Longer kisses ⟶ Sexual touches ⟶ Sexual intercourse

Point out that progress along the line might be spread out over weeks, months, and years, or it might be condensed into one night. Explain that it is natural for a man to move much more rapidly along the line than a woman.

B. The continuum can be looked at in two ways

1. On the purely physical level—as the natural biological steps that lead to intercourse (luv only).

2. On the personal level—as progressive *signs* that express a developing *love* relationship.

The question is: when are the signs "good" and when are they "bad"? Or better: when does "good" end and "bad" begin? The class will see readily that the signs are bad when they are not really signs of love, but just using the other person to get sexual gratification. The problem is: when are they bad when they truly are signs of love? The key to the answer is in the word "truly." A kiss is good if it is a true sign of the love I have for this person. Intercourse is a true sign if it means I love this person so much that I am willing to give my whole life to him or her. Obviously, then, intercourse is true only in marriage. (An older group might want to dispute this point. If so, save it for another class when you have time to develop the reasons for it. A younger group will accept it at face value.)

C. We still haven't answered the question: how far can we go? If the movement along the continuum were even and controlled, it would be easy to answer. The signs would progress as the love grew, and there would be no problem. However, we all know that's not the way it is. The progress on the line looks something like the chart on the following page. For awhile you are running along on level ground. You are in control and can stop anytime you want. Then suddenly, you are running straight downhill. You are no longer in control of the situation. You can't stop even if you want to. Your brakes snap. Unless some external force intervenes, you are on your way to intercourse.

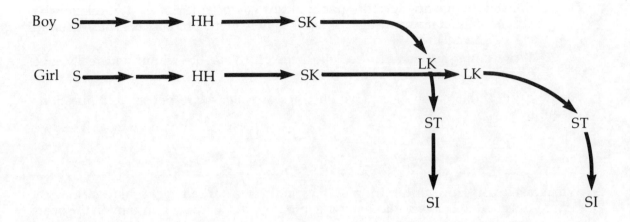

Point out the difference between the boy's braking point and the girl's. Emphasize the difficulty a girl will have in stopping a boy once he has started downhill. Help the students to see that the brakes must be applied when both are still in control of the situation. The sex drive is a powerful instinct. Given its freedom, it can wipe out training, resolutions, responsibility, self-respect, respect for another.

Talk to the girls about sexual teasing—stringing a boy along, past his braking point, and then turning him off. Point out to the boys that the girl will not be aroused as easily as he. If he waits for her to call a halt, it may be too late for him.

D. What are the brakes that we use to control this powerful human instinct?

- The best control is a C or D relationship. If there is respect and trust and real love in a relationship, it is not as likely to get out of hand.
- Parental rules are meant to be a control. Parents were teens once, too. Their rules reflect their knowledge of the kinds of situations that can lead to sexual trouble. If kids object, "Don't you trust me?" the answer should be: I trust you, but I don't trust the sexual drive that is a part of you. Parent rules should be explained and then enforced.
- Chaperones. An unchaperoned party is very likely to get out of hand. Why?

E. Give out slips of paper for anonymous responses and questions.

Session 5 — Where do you go from here?

A. Explain to the teens that the teen years are the time of life in which they must learn to integrate luv and love. Being in love (luv) is one of the most exciting things they will ever experience, but it is not the greatest. It takes time to sort all this out in their minds. It takes time to get their sexuality under control, to learn to use their sexuality as a sign of love, as a beautiful gift.

B. Review the three psychological persons taught in a previous lesson. (See Unit 2) Point out that each of these "persons"—all of whom are a part of you—responds differently to the question of sexuality.

Child: The psychological child says GO. The child is curious, wants to try everything, touches what he is told not to touch, uses others, is impatient, wants satisfaction now, likes to be cuddled. Your child wants to play the game of sex, NOW. Luv is located mainly in the child.

Parent: The psychological parent says NO. The "parent" is the part of you that contains the rules and regulations about sex that have been pounded into your minds since childhood. Most of these are negative rules: don't touch, don't look, don't park, don't flirt, don't wear tight clothing, don't drink.

Adult: The psychological adult says SLOW. The adult is the part of you that understands sexuality and how it operates. In the adult are located respect and love. The adult in you knows how powerful the sex drive is and doesn't get into dangerous situations.

C. Explain that the purpose of this unit has been to strengthen the adult in regard to sexuality. However, at the same time, the classes have been arousing the curiosity of the child. As a teacher you have taken the risk that someone in the class with a poorly formed adult will take these lessons just on the child level. For such a student, the classes would be a source of temptation rather than a help. Ask the students to react to that problem. Was the risk justified?

D. At this stage in a teen's life both the parent and the adult are needed to keep the child under control. The "parent" is usually backed by some external force: parents, chaperones. Discuss with the class what happens to most teens if left in a situation where only their adult, without any external parental control, is trying to control the child: e.g., a parked car, or an empty cottage.

E. One of the biggest problems concerning sex is drinking. Help the teens to see why this is so. What does drinking do to the parent? (It dulls it, turns it off. This is precisely why people drink—to get rid of the pressures that the psychological parent puts on us.) What does drinking do to the adult? (It confuses the adult. The reasoning part of us does not function right under the influence of alcohol or other drugs. This is the effect of drinking that the drinker doesn't want, tries to deny, but can't avoid.) What does drinking do to the child? (Drinking frees the child. The child is the spontaneous fun-loving part of us. However, the child is also the selfish, inconsiderate part of us.) Help the class to see why their parents and others who love them are so concerned about drinking on dates. The child is hard enough to control when the parent and adult are in full command. When they are turned off and confused, what is left to apply the brakes?

F. Teen years are filled with dangers to sexual integrity. It is important to make sure that there are also plenty of safeguards. Write at the board DANGERS and SAFEGUARDS. Have the class list several of each. Collate answers. Then ask the students to code each thing listed to show how much of a danger or safeguard it is for them. Use a scale of one to three. Some possible items for the lists are given below:

Dangers: drinking, parking, older friends, curiosity, unchaperoned parties, peer pressures, movies, sex books and magazines, popularity

Safeguards: sports, studies, good friends, parents, laughter, things to do, adult friend, prayer, confession, good fun

G. Give out papers for questions and responses.

Session 6 — Matrimony—sexuality on the sacramental level

A. Explain again that sexual intercourse can be thought of simply as a biological act, it can be seen as a beautiful sign of love between two persons, or it can be seen as a sacrament an integral part of the sacrament of matrimony. As a sacrament it is one of the seven special ways God has chosen to give himself to mankind.

We can think of a man simply as an animal. (Draw stick-man.) Or we can think of him as an animal body in which a free and loving person lives. (Draw an oval to represent the person.) Or we can think of him as a person in whom God dwells. (Draw a triangle to represent the presence of God in the person.)

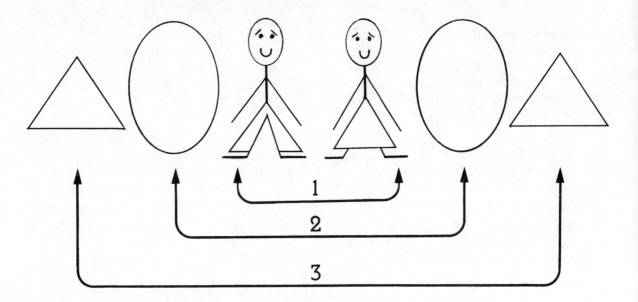

So we can think of sex as:

1) Biology—the reproductive action between the male and female of the human species; a source of physical pleasure.
2) Personal sign—a means of communication between two persons; through the physical act of intercourse these two persons tell one another of their total love and commitment.
3) Sacrament—a means of growing in grace; the loving Christian couple can give God to one another by their act of love. Just as a person is holier after receiving communion or the sacrament of reconciliation, that person is holier, closer to God after giving him or herself in love to the marriage partner.

B. Matrimony is a decision:

—to spend a lifetime working on developing a love relationship with one special person.
—to give oneself completely to that person, to let no other relationship come between you and the loved one.
—to accept, love, and care for whatever children will result from the union.
—to help the person you love grow in the love of God.

Point out that unless that last element is present, you have a marriage but not the sacrament of matrimony. Some priests will not perform the marriage ceremony unless they are assured that the couple is really serious about including God in their marriage. Discuss this with the class.

C. Have students list the kind of qualities they would be looking for in a marriage partner. Share responses.

D. Explain religious life as it fits into this idea of marriage: Just as marriage is a decision to spend a lifetime developing one primary love-relationship, religious life is a decision to spend a lifetime developing the relationship with God. The person who marries promises that he will let no luv relationship distract him from his love (and luv) for his spouse. The religious promises the same. The religious promises not to foster any luv relationships in order to be free to develop love relationships with all the people he serves. (This topic could easily be developed into an entire lesson.)

E. Give out papers for responses and questions.

Session 7 — On premarital sex (for more mature classes)

A. The church, your parents, society all say that sex before marriage is wrong. The movies you see, the books you read, the songs you sing, the general attitude of the younger generation, your own feelings all seem to imply that sex before marriage is good. How do <u>you</u> decide?

B. A sensible decision can be made only after we have looked at both sides of the situation. Work out together some reasons <u>for</u> premarital sex and some reasons <u>against</u> it. Discuss the decision in terms of these reasons.

Reasons FOR: (These are typical of those given by society. Of course, you as a teacher of religion most likely do not agree with them.)
1. Practice makes perfect.
2. Find out if we're really suited for each other.
3. We really love one another.
4. The experience of sex makes you grow up.
5. We both want it so why not.
6. It's fun.
7. Everybody does it these days.

Reasons AGAINST:
1. Intercourse is a sign of complete commitment. There is no assurance of this before marriage.
2. Possibility of pregnancy.
3. Too much too soon can destroy a real love relationship.
4. Chance of psychological damage, especially for the girl.
5. Sexual intimacy must be learned—can only be learned in a permanent relationship.
6. If people run around before marriage—they'll run around after.
7. Religions teach that it is a serious sin. This teaching is meant to protect the sacredness of marriage and to protect the rights of individuals.
8. Society is against it—parents are against it.

9. Weakens or destroys self-respect.
10. Venereal disease.

The reasons listed above are not in any special order. Discuss them and any others your students may add.

C. Review the six levels of morality taught in Unit 2. How would a person who operated on each of these levels answer the question: "Should I or shouldn't I?" What reasons for saying "yes" or for saying "no" would a person give who was following a level one morality? level two?

D. Give out papers for questions and responses to the whole unit.

Feedback Starters

The following is a list of sample sentence starters to use for introductory or feedback sessions.

I can experience God best when...
What bugs me most about *the church* is... (school, my parents, my friends)
I really wish that...
What I don't understand about *confession* is... (baptism, this class, you, myself)
That lesson really made sense because...
That lesson didn't make sense because...
I am dissatisfied with *the church* because... (this class, my grades, my family)
I am angry with _____ because...
I am grateful to *my parents* for... (the church, my teachers, my country)
If I were *Pope* I would... (pastor, principal, teaching this class)
The thing I liked *best* about this class so far was... (least)
I think this class could be improved by...
I know I will have to work at...
I have really made up my mind to...
I was surprised to discover that...
I am sorry that...
The most important thing I *learned* today was... (did, tried, wanted)
I'm still confused about...
I'd like to spend more time on...
I would like to ask (tell) *Mary Jo* that... (the teacher, the whole class)
I (always, usually, seldom) attend Sunday Mass because...
I (often, seldom, never) attend weekday Mass because...
My biggest problem with the Mass is...
If for some reason I miss Sunday Mass, I _____ to make up for it.

Tear - Out Section

The following are duplicates of pages found within the text. They are perforated for your convenience in copying the material for distribution in class.

I am not as close to God as I should be because:

1) I don't take time to think about the deeper realities of life: who I am, where I fit in the world, what happens after death, what is really right and wrong.

2) I think about these things, but I don't relate the answers to God.

3) I want to be my own God. I don't want to have to be responsible to anyone but myself for what I do with my life.

4) I am afraid of facing God. He might not like me, or he might find fault with the way I am living my life. He might ask me to change something I don't want to change.

5) I have too many mixed up ideas about God. The God I experience doesn't fit in with God as I learn about him.

6) I don't need God. I can take care of myself.

Parable of the Unknown God

Once upon a mountaintop there lived
a kind and gentle god. In Shula Hi,
a village far below, his people lived.
They were a very busy people: many
books to read and many games to play,
and very many meetings to attend.

The Shula Hians seldom thought about
the kind and gentle god. So far away
he seemed. No one had ever seen his face.
Some doubted he was even there at all.

Yet, day by day the gentle god looked down
upon his own, and wanted very much
that they should be his friends. I must, he thought,
do some small thing to show them that I care.
And so each day he sent a messenger
to Shula Hi, a pack upon his back,
and in the pack he bore a special gift,
a gift for every person in the land.

Each day the gifts would come. Each day the people
ran with open arms to gather them.
But soon they grew quite used to being gifted.
Some began to grab gifts from the pack,
And some took more than they were meant to have,
and some complained of gifts that were too small.
At last no one remembered who the gifts
were from. And no one even thought to ask.

And far up on his mountaintop sat god.
Day after lonely day he waited
for a friendly word, a word of thanks, or just
a word that said, "Hi, god, I know you're there."

But no word came. The Shula Hians took
the gifts as if they had a right to them
and more. But god? Well, he was far away.
And some said, "What's he ever done for me?"
And some, "I don't believe he even is."

If I can't tell them that I am, god thought,
how can I tell that I am a friend
and want to give them friendship most of all?

And then his eyes lit up, "I know," he said,
"I'll give a party for my friends below.
I'll give a party and invite them all.
And surely if they spend some time with me,
and learn to know how much I really care,
oh, surely then they'll know I am their friend."

And so the invitations were sent out.
A list was posted on the town house wall
for all who wished to come to sign their names.

The Shula Hians saw the invitation.
Some just laughed and said, "That's not for me!"
And some said, "Spend a day with god? No way!"
And some were very busy with their chores
and said, "Some other time but not today."
And some were tempted: "Maybe it's for real,
and maybe god does want to be my friend."
And timidly they signed up for the day.
But when the others laughed they were ashamed
and found excuses why they couldn't go.

The party day arrived, but no one went.

And in his mountain home the kind god sat.
"I only want to give them love," he said.
"How can I tell them? Make them understand?
Is there not one who wants me for a friend?"

And in the village far below, the Shula Hians
laughed and cried and worked and played and died.
And seldom thought about the gentle god,
and did not know he loved them very much,
and did not know he loved . . .
and did not know.

Sister Kieran Sawyer

1. Spanking level - to avoid punishment

2. Lollipop level - to get a reward

3. Good boy (girl) level - to get approval (of parents, friends, society)

4. Play-by-the-rules level - to keep the rules (of life, of the family, of the country)

5. Conviction level - to do the right thing

6. Love level - to help someone in need, out of unselfish concern for all others.

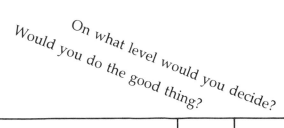

You have to decide if you will...

	On what level would you decide?	Would you do the good thing?
1. steal $10.00 left on a teacher's desk		
2. tell your parents the truth about a fender dented while leaving a beer party		
3. speak respectfully to parents scolding you about your brother's mistake		
4. go to school when you feel like faking sick		
5. give your brother a birthday present — he didn't give you one		
6. give money to the missions		
7. go to classes — three good friends are skipping and want you to come		
8. not cheat on a math test — you're sitting next to the class brain		
9. go to Mass on Sunday and participate when you get there		
10. make your bed and clean your room		
11. do your assignments neatly		
12. talk to an unpopular student in the cafeteria		
13. stick up for an unpopular teacher when the other students are cutting him (her) down		
14. listen respectfully to your parents' explanation of the way things were "back then"		
15. report a serious act of vandalism		
16. not go to a party — you know if you go you'll get bombed		
17. quit drinking completely or cut down to one or two beers		
18. help a teacher carry some things or set up the gym		
19. attend a prayer meeting		
20. go to daily Mass		

Three psychological persons can be found within each person:

The Psychological Parent	The Psychological Adult	The Psychological Child
1. Represents the *taught* concepts in life.	1. Represents the *thought* concepts.	1. Represents the *felt* concepts.
2. The psychological parent: 　pressures 　blames 　finds fault 　gives orders 　domineers	2. The psychological adult: 　figures things out 　solves problems 　weighs consequences 　understands 　thinks things through	2. The psychological child: 　plays 　pouts 　laughs 　cries 　explores
3. The parent is: 　strict 　uncompromising 　inconsistent 　protective	3. The adult is: 　aware 　creative 　responsible 　thoughtful	3. The child is: 　spontaneous 　curious 　charming 　playful 　demanding 　jealous 　carefree 　pouty
4. In the psychological parent are found: 　laws 　regulations 　sanctions 　prejudices 　taboos 　threats 　social pressures	4. In the psychological adult are found: 　values 　ideas 　realities 　truths	4. In the psychological child are found: 　wishes 　fears 　feelings 　guilts 　delights 　frustrations
5. In regard to others the parent: 　protects (overly) 　dominates 　blames 　finds fault	5. In regard to others the adult: 　understands 　trusts 　loves	5. In regard to others the child: 　enjoys 　uses 　manipulates 　takes advantage of
6. Sources of the parent are: 　parents 　teachers 　older children 　TV	6. Sources of the adult are: 　experience 　examined data from the parent or the child	6. Sources of the child are: 　felt reactions to people, and experiences

What is a Christian?

A Christian is a person who

_____believes in God

_____believes in the Blessed Trinity

_____believes that Jesus Christ is God

_____believes that Jesus died for human beings and rose again

_____believes that Jesus lives now in our midst

_____accepts Jesus as a personal friend and savior

_____prays to the Father as Jesus taught

_____keeps the ten commandments and Jesus' commandments of love

_____tries to live according to the teachings of Jesus:

   —to love God above all

   —to love others as ourselves

   —to forgive our enemies

   —to care for the poor and lowly

   —to treat all people as brothers and sisters

What is a Catholic Christian?

A Catholic Christian is one who, *besides* the things listed above:

_____accepts the Pope as Christ's representative on earth

_____celebrates the eucharist every Sunday with other Catholics

_____believes that Jesus is present in the eucharist

_____receives Holy Communion during the Easter time

_____confesses at least once a year

_____contributes to the support of the church

_____believes that the best way to live the Christian life is within the Catholic Church

_____receives the sacraments within the Catholic Church

BREAD OF LIFE (John 6: 22–69)

Narrator: It is the day after the multiplication of the loaves. Most of us were there yesterday. We were part of the crowd that the man Jesus fed with just five loaves of bread and two fish. We wanted to bring Jesus back with us to the city to make him our king, but he didn't want that. He went up into the mountain and hid from the crowd. Later that evening some ot us saw his disciples leaving in the boat without him. This morning we've all gathered in the marketplace to see what new developments have happened. Everyone is still talking about the miracle of the bread and fish. Suddenly, Jesus arrives in the marketplace.

First Person: Here he comes now.

Second Person: How did he get across the lake? He didn't leave in the boat with his followers.

Third Person: I took the last boat home. He didn't come with me.

Fourth Person: (Addressing Jesus) Sir, where did you disappear to yesterday? We were looking all over the mountainside for you.

Jesus: (Sadly) Yes, you were looking for me. But only because I fed you. Not because you believe in me. You shouldn't be so concerned about perishable things like food. No, spend your energies seeking the eternal life that the Son of Man can give you. For God the Father has sent me for this very purpose.

Fifth person: What do we have to do to please God?

Jesus: What God wants is this: That you believe in the one he has sent to you.

Sixth Person: You must show us more miracles if you want us to believe in you.

First Person: Sure, just give us free bread every day, like our fathers had while they journeyed in the wilderness.

Second Person: Yeah, like it says in the holy book, "Moses gave them bread from heaven."

Jesus: Moses didn't give it to them. My Father did. And now he offers you the true bread from heaven. The true bread is a person—the one sent by God from heaven, and he gives life to the world.

Third Person: Sir, if that's true, give us this bread every day of our lives.

Jesus: I am the bread of life. No one coming to me will ever be hungry again. Those believing in me will never thirst.

Narrator: Then the Jews began murmuring and grumbling to themselves because he claimed to be the Bread from heaven.
(Everyone murmurs and grumbles.)

Fourth Person:	What's he talking about? He is merely Jesus the son of Joseph, we know his father and mother; we know where he is from.
Fifth Person:	What is he trying to say? We know he didn't come down from heaven.
Jesus:	Don't murmur among yourselves about my saying that. Those the Father speaks to, who learn the truth from him, will understand. Yes, I am the bread of life. There was no real life in that bread from the skies which was given to your fathers in the wilderness, for they all died. But there is such a thing as bread from heaven that will give eternal life to everyone who eats it. And I am that living bread. Anyone who eats this bread will live forever; my flesh is this bread, given to the world.
Narrator:	Then the Jews began arguing with each other about what he meant. (Everyone talks—some are getting angry.)
Sixth Person:	How can this man give us his flesh to eat?
Jesus:	With all the earnestness I possess I tell you this: Unless you eat the flesh of the son of man and drink his blood, you cannot have eternal life within you. My flesh is the true food, and my blood is the true drink. Everyone who eats my flesh and drinks my blood lives in me and I live in him.
First Person:	This is very hard to understand.
Second Person:	Who can tell what he means?
Third Person:	This teaching is too hard.
Fourth Person:	Who can listen to this?
Narrator:	Jesus knew that his disciples were confused and some were gumbling and complaining.
Jesus:	Some of you do not believe. That is what I meant when I said that no one can come to me unless the Father speaks to his heart.
Narrator:	At this point many of his disciples turned away and did not follow him anymore. (Most of the crowd get up and walk away, shaking their heads in disgust. A few stay near Jesus.)
Narrator:	Jesus watched them walk away. Then he turned to the Twelve.
Jesus:	And you—are you going to leave me also?
Narrator:	Peter answered for them all.
Peter:	Master, to whom would we go? You alone have the words that give eternal life. And we believe that you are the holy Son of God.

The Little Prince (excerpts)

It was then that the fox appeared.

"Good morning," said the fox.

"Good morning," the little prince responded politely, although when he turned around he saw nothing.

"I am right here," the voice said, "under the apple tree."

"Who are you?" asked the little prince, and added, "You are very pretty to look at."

"I am a fox," the fox said.

"Come and play with me," proposed the little prince. "I am so unhappy."

"I cannot play with you," the fox said. "I am not tamed."

"Ah! Please excuse me," said the little prince.

But, after some thought, he added:

"What does that mean—'tame'?"

. . . .

"It is an act too often neglected," said the fox. "It means to establish ties."

"'To establish ties'?"

"Just that," said the fox. "To me, you are still nothing more than a little boy who is just like a hundred thousand other little boys. And I have no need of you. And you, on your part, have no need of me. To you, I am nothing more than a fox like a hundred thousand other foxes. But if you tame me, then we shall need each other. To me, you will be unique in all the world. To you, I shall be unique in all the world..."

"I am beginning to understand," said the little prince. "There is a flower... I think that she has tamed me..."

"It is possible," said the fox. "On the earth one sees all sorts of things."

. . . .

But he came back to his idea.

"My life is very monotonous," he said. "I hunt chickens; men hunt me. All the chickens are just alike, and all the men are just alike. And, in consequence, I am a little bored. But if you tame me, it will be as if the sun came to shine on my life. I shall know the sound of a step that will be different from all the others. Other steps send me hurrying back underneath the ground. Yours will call me, like music, out of my burrow. And then look: you see the grain-fields down yonder? I do not eat bread. Wheat is of no use to me. The wheat fields have nothing to say to me. And that is sad. But you have hair that is the color of gold. Think how wonderful that will be when you have tamed me! The grain, which is also golden, will bring me back the thought of you. And I shall love to listen to the wind in the wheat..."

The fox gazed at the little prince, for a long time.

"Please, tame me!" he said.

"I want to very much," the little prince replied. "But I have not much time. I have friends to discover and a great many things to understand."

"One only understands the things that one tames," said the fox. "Men have no more time to understand anything. They buy things all ready made at the shops. But there is no shop anywhere where one can buy friendship, and so men have no friends any more. If you want a friend, tame me..."

"What must I do, to tame you?" asked the little prince.

"You must be very patient," replied the fox. "First you will sit down at a little distance from me—like that—in the grass. I shall look at you out of the corner of

my eye, and you will say nothing. Words are the source of misunderstandings. But you will sit a little closer to me, every day..."

. . . .

So the little prince tamed the fox. And when the hour of his departure drew near—

"Ah," said the fox, "I shall cry."

"It is your own fault," said the little prince. "I never wished you any sort of harm, but you wanted me to tame you..."

"Yes, that is so," said the fox.

"But now you are going to cry!" said the little prince.

"Yes, that is so," said the fox.

"Then it has done no good at all!"

"It has done me good," said the fox, "because of the color of the wheat fields." And then he added:

"Go and look again at the roses. You will understand now that yours is unique in all the world. Then come back to say goodbye to me, and I will make you a present of a secret."

The little prince went away to look again at the roses.

"You are not at all like my rose," he said. "As yet you are nothing. No one has tamed you, and you have tamed no one. You are like my fox when I first knew him. He was only a fox like a hundred thousand other foxes. But I have made him my friend, and now he is unique in all the world."

And the roses were very much embarrassed.

"You are beautiful, but you are empty," he went on. "One could not die for you. To be sure an ordinary passerby would think that my rose looked just like you—the rose that belongs to me. But in herself alone she is more important than all the hundreds of other roses: because it is she that I have watered; because it is she that I have put under the glass globe; because it is she that I have sheltered behind the screen; because it is for her that I have killed the caterpillars (except the two or three that we saved to become butterflies); because it is she that I have listened to, when she grumbled, or boasted, or even sometimes when she said nothing. Because she is *my* rose."

And he went back to meet the fox.

"Goodbye," he said.

"Goodbye," said the fox. "And now here is my secret, a very simple secret: It is only with the heart that one can see rightly; what is essential is invisible to the eye."

"What is essential is invisible to the eye," the little prince repeated, so that he would be sure to remember.

. . . .

To be a whole human being, every person needs:	SELF Persons who respect this quality in themselves would:	OTHERS Persons who respect this quality in others would:

GOD	The most basic relationship with God requires one to:

Jesus elevated the whole moral code to three simple rules:

LOVE GOD   LOVE SELF   LOVE OTHERS

Personal Integrity
(the person in himself)

FREEDOM
I want to be a person who
_____ is really free
_____ makes his own decisions
_____ has his own set of values
_____ stands up for what he believes
_____ is independent
_____ has strong will-power

TRUTH
I want to be a person who
_____ knows the truth about himself
_____ knows the truth about his world
_____ understands his God and religion
_____ is able to reason out problems
_____ has a good education
_____ can accept failure
_____ is honest with himself
_____ is open to new ideas
_____ admits his own mistakes
_____ says what he means

LIFE AND SEXUALITY
I want to be a person who
_____ is mentally and physically whole
_____ has a healthy body
_____ has a healthy mind
_____ doesn't overdo it
_____ is good looking
_____ understands his own sexuality
_____ respects his own body
_____ has control of his sexual self

PROPERTY
I want to be a person who
_____ has things he can call his own
_____ is financially set
_____ has a good career or job
_____ has the kind of house, car, clothes he wants

LOVE OF SELF
I want to be a person who
_____ has many true friends
_____ gets along well with others

_____ is well-adjusted
_____ has a good sense of humor
_____ is able to influence others
_____ is loved
_____ is treated with respect
_____ is easy-going and carefree
_____ has a don't quit attitude
_____ gives his best at everything
_____ is successful
_____ is somebody
_____ is real, not fake
_____ has no enemies

Justice and Love
(the person in relationship)

GOD: ACKNOWLEDGE, RESPECT, WORSHIP
I want to be a person who
_____ acknowledges God as his Lord
_____ really prays
_____ is grateful to God for everything
_____ worships God freely and lovingly
_____ wants to know God better
_____ is close to God
_____ gives a gift of himself to God
_____ lives the Christian life fully
_____ respects God's name, buildings
_____ accepts God's help in his life

OTHERS: RESPECT FOR FREEDOM AND AUTHORITY
I want to be a person who
_____ respects the freedom of every person
_____ respects and loves his parents
_____ respects church authorities
_____ respects teachers, policemen, and others in authority.
_____ obeys the laws of city and country,
_____ is just
_____ works with others

RESPECT FOR LIFE AND SEXUALITY
I want to be a person who
_____ respects all human life
_____ protects nature and wildlife,

_____ drives safely
_____ is careful of water, air, and land
_____ respects the sexuality of others
_____ respects the contract of marriage

RESPECT FOR PROPERTY
I want to be a person who
_____ respects the property of others
_____ takes care of public property
_____ does not steal or damage property
_____ pays his share (taxes, dues)

RESPECT FOR TRUTH
I want to be a person who
_____ can be trusted
_____ tells the truth
_____ is honest in his dealings with others

LOVE OF OTHERS
I want to be a person who
_____ gives of himself for others
_____ respects the feelings of others
_____ is kind and considerate
_____ is unselfish
_____ is grateful
_____ cares for the sick, lonely, deprived
_____ brings joy to others
_____ believes in others
_____ listens
_____ cares
_____ knows how to really love

+ building going well
– building going poorly
0 not in my plans at all

Is the bible true?

That question can only be answered if we understand that there are different kinds of truth.

RELIGIOUS TRUTH — The bible is primarily religious truth. Religion is concerned with man's relationship with God, and the bible is the record of the relationship between God and his chosen people, the Hebrews. It tells how God treated them and how they responded (or failed to respond) to him.

MORAL TRUTH — The bible also contains much moral truth. Moral truth tells us what is right and wrong, what we must do and how we must live if we want to be good people and close to God. However, the Old Testament reflects the morality of the Hebrew people, and their standards were very different from ours. For instance, according to Hebrew morality, if a person poked out your eye, you were permitted to poke out one of his, if he knocked out your tooth, you could knock out one of his. The New Testament tells us that Jesus expressly raised the moral standards. "It was said of old . . . , but I say to you. . . ."

SYMBOLIC TRUTH — Much of the truth in scripture is told in symbols, parables, myths and allegories. We have to read between the lines to discover the truth being presented. The story of the tree of good and evil is an example of such a symbol. There is truth there, but it is religious truth, not factual truth about apples and snakes.

PROVERBIAL TRUTH — Much of the bible, especially the Wisdom books, is the kind of folksy truth contained in proverbs, like: Do unto others as you would have others do unto you; A stitch in times saves nine.

HISTORICAL TRUTH — The bible contains the history of the Hebrew people from about 2000 BC to 100 AD. Though much of this history was passed down orally for generations before it was written, it is, nonetheless, surprisingly accurate. There are, however, some historical errors in the bible.

SCIENTIFIC TRUTH — The biblical writers reflect the scientific understandings of their day, which—we now know—were very primitive. For instance, the bible describes the earth as flat, says the sun stood still, says the world was created in seven days. We are able to read right through the scientific errors in the bible and find the religious truth the writer was trying to get across. There was no need for God to reveal a more accurate understanding of science to his people. Revelation is concerned with religious truth not scientific truth. The Hebrew people didn't have to know that the world was round in order to be close to God.

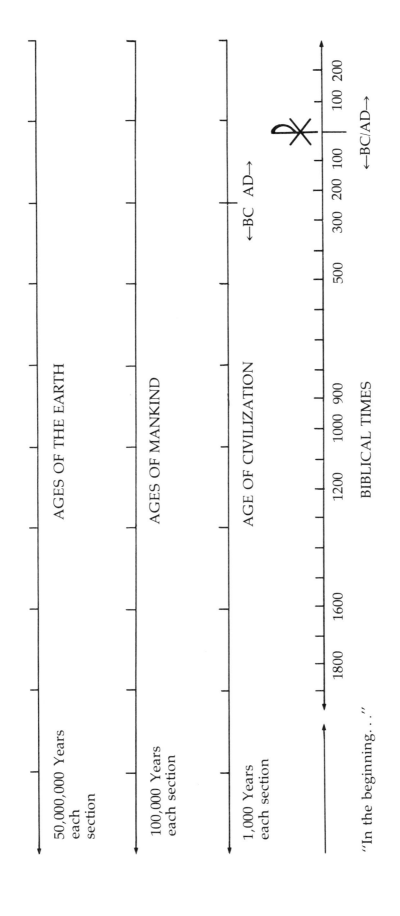

AGES OF THE EARTH

50,000,000 Years
each
section

AGES OF MANKIND

100,000 Years
each section

AGE OF CIVILIZATION

←BC AD→

1,000 Years
each section

BIBLICAL TIMES

1800 1600 1200 1000 900 500 300 200 100 100 200

←BC/AD→

"In the beginning..."

A man went out to plant his seed...	Name the "sowers" in your life—the persons who have planted the Word of God in your soil.	Some seed fell on the path—the birds ate it before it ever sprouted...	In your life, who or what are the "birds" that snatch the seed of God away before it gets a chance?
Some fell on rocky ground. The soil wasn't deep enough—the plants soon dried up...	What might cause a person to be rocky soil—one who hears the word, begins to practice it, but soon gives up?	Some fell among thorns which grew up and choked the plants.	What are the thorns in your life—the worries or desires or riches that grow with the seed and crowd Christ out?

Some fell in good ground.	What definite things could you <u>do</u> each day to keep the seeds of Christianity growing and yielding fruit in your life? List 5.

Put a star next to the one of these things that you have definitely decided you <u>will</u> do.

JESUS PRESENTS A CONTINUUM IN THIS PARABLE. CAN YOU PLACE YOUR-SELF ON IT?

X	X	X	X	X	X
hardened ground—no growth	thin soil no roots— growth doesn't last	rich soil— but too many weeds	30-fold	60-fold	100-fold